THE NEW YORKER BOOK OF VERSE

The NEW YORKER
BOOK OF VERSE

An Anthology

OF POEMS FIRST PUBLISHED

IN THE NEW YORKER

1925-1935

HARCOURT, BRACE AND COMPANY

NEW YORK

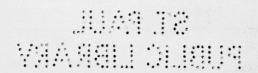

PRINTED IN THE UNITED STATES OF AMERICA
BY QUINN & BODEN COMPANY, INC., RAHWAY, N. J.
Typography by Robert Josephy

CONTENTS

v

II. FEBRUARY: *The fountain is dry at the Plaza*

III. MARCH: *With a scud of storm*

IV. APRIL: *It is Spring! It is Spring!*
On the lea, on the ling!

viii

v. MAY: *Birds toot sweet on every bough*

VI. JUNE: *At summer's brink*

VII. JULY: *Music on the Mall*

VIII. AUGUST: *Dozes the town*

IX. SEPTEMBER: *A scarlet leaf*

xiv

Foreword

The publishers have selected the three hundred poems in this book, by God knows what wayward processes, from more than four thousand which appeared in the first ten years' issues of *The New Yorker*. (The four thousand, to get into really paralyzing statistics, were selected by the editors of the magazine from more than ninety thousand which found their way, with and without return postage, into their offices during the same period.) Beyond the fact that all three hundred once managed to get the approval of a group of editors noted for their strong and often irrational prejudices, these poems have nothing much in common. *The New Yorker* being what it is, a good many are funny, or as their creators must prefer to dream, satirical. Others are thoughtful, indignant, or just sad. One is in French, and, as somebody in the publisher's office remarked in a little note accompanying the galley proofs, several others might just as well be.

Almost all carry with them the memory of ancient conflicts between author and editor—the editor zealous to put in commas and clear things up generally; the author fierce to guard his unpunctuated rhythms, the ingenious mysteries of his thought. These struggles have resulted through the years in an agitated, technical, and highly articulate correspondence, often at least as interesting as the poems themselves, and it is the publisher's misfortune that none of it can be reproduced here, if only to give the reader some notion of the fury which goes into the production of even the briefest lyric composition.

From the contributor's point of view this anthology is unique. Some time ago a commentator in the magazine wrote:

"The commonly accepted practice, when a man has an idea for collecting other people's published works into a volume, is for him to write his authors inviting them into the book and, if he mentions the subject of pay at all, offering to settle out of court, so to speak, for a small sum. For the privilege of using such articles or stories as are controlled by the publications which first published them, he meets whatever inflexible demands the publications choose to make. For all others, he deals directly with the authors, who usually are as flexible as a willow rod. Occasionally an old, surly author will snap back at an anthologist; but for the most part authors glow with pride at getting reprinted and ask for nothing but the glory. . . .

"A book is a gamble: some books don't sell, others sell like the very devil. The authors, as well as the anthologist, should be in on the gamble—if only for the somehow unforgettable reason that they were the folks who actually wrote the darn stuff."

This book has been assembled on this last basis—except that no share of the royalties has been reserved for an anthologist. Every author is to be paid his strictly pro-rata share of the profits, according to the amount of space his verse takes up. It is difficult to believe that this policy can be of the slightest interest to the casual reader, and it is mentioned here only for the information of the creative artist generally, and the embarrassment of other, and less high-minded, anthologists.

The New Yorker Book of Verse contains poems by more than one hundred contributors, almost all of whom will be familiar to readers of poetry. A few names, however, may seem a little startling. Ring Lardner is represented, for instance, and so is Rollin Kirby, and it was only with the greatest reluctance that the publishers decided not to include a verse by Joseph V. McKee, who at the time he wrote was Acting Mayor and wished to sing in defense of municipal statuary.

The publishers, finally, are very proud of the arrangement of this book, which is seasonal rather than topical or emotional. The poems, that is, are divided into twelve sections, one for each month, so that the reader, in a soft May mood, can get May poetry without skipping around. The editors of the magazine, who obviously cannot comment on the quality of the verse in this collection, can and do express their admiration for such ingenuities as this, and for the courage and energy involved in compiling such a book at all. THE NEW YORKER

Acknowledgments

Thanks are due to many publishers whose generous coöperation has made this anthology possible. This indebtedness is specifically acknowledged to: ALBERT & CHARLES BONI, INC. for "City Songs" by Mark Van Doren from *Now the Sky;* COWARD-MCCANN, INC. for the poems by Alfred Kreymborg from *Manhattan Men;* DODD, MEAD & COMPANY for the poems by William Rose Benét from *Golden Fleece,* and for "An Alley Cat" by Nancy Byrd Turner from *A Riband on My Rein;* DORRANCE & COMPANY, INC. for "Portrait" by Isabel McLennan McMeekin from *Contemporary Poets of Dorrance,* Volume 131; DOUBLEDAY, DORAN & COMPANY for nine poems by Phyllis McGinley from *On the Contrary,* and for "Epigrams in a Cellar" by Christopher Morley from *Poems;* E. P. DUTTON & COMPANY, INC. for poems by Margaret Fishback from *I Feel Better Now, Out of My Head,* and *I Take It Back;* HARPER & BROTHERS for eight poems by E. B. White from *The Lady Is Cold;* HOUGHTON MIFFLIN COMPANY for "Unfinished History" by Archibald MacLeish from *Poems: 1924-1933,* for the poems by Elspeth from *Young Man, Beware* and *Strange Truth,* and for five poems by Frances Frost; ALFRED A. KNOPF, INC. for the poems by Elinor Wylie from *The Collected Poems of Elinor Wylie,* for "Knockout" by Charles Norman from *Poems,* and for "Tu Ne Quaesieris" by Clinch Calkins from *Poems;* LIVERIGHT PUBLISHING CORPORATION for selections from *Enough Rope* and *Sunset Gun* by Dorothy Parker, and for three poems by Samuel Hoffenstein; THE MACMILLAN COMPANY for two poems by Elizabeth Coatsworth from *Away Goes Sally,* for the poem by Robert P. Tristram Coffin from *Strange Holiness,* and for two poems by Mark Van Doren from *A Winter Diary;* ROBERT M. MC BRIDE & COMPANY for four poems by Peggy Bacon; THOMAS B. MOSHER for "Susanna Passes" by Sydney King Russell from *Lost Warrior;* G. P. PUTNAM'S SONS for two Sob

Ballads by Clarence Knapp from *I'm Sorry If I Have Offended;* CHARLES SCRIBNER'S SONS for poems by David McCord from *The Crows* and *Bay Window Ballads;* SIMON & SCHUSTER, INC., for the poems by Ogden Nash from *Hard Lines, Free Wheeling, Happy Days,* and *The Primrose Path;* THE VIKING PRESS for "Tombstones in the Starlight" and "Little Words" from *Death and Taxes* by Dorothy Parker; THE YALE UNIVERSITY PRESS for poems by Clarence Day from *Scenes from the Mesozoic,* and for the poem by Dorothy Belle Flanagan from *Dark Certainty.*

1. JANUARY: *Visibly a little frost*

The Prodigal

O silver city, though you be in truth
My spirit's home, the temple of my youth,
Yet I have ever tried in vain to love
You with a splendid and a perfect love.
Your strength I boast, your unassailable pride,
The countless spears in your unwounded side,
Your cruelty and your magnificence,
Your barbarism and your ignorance.
Yet for the things you lack, the gallantry,
The erudition and philosophy,
I have renounced you time on time, and fled,
Only to hasten back with lowered head.
Having so longed to love you to excess,
And failed and failed, I thought to love you less,
And tore your gaudy colors from my breast,
Saying, "The lands of long ago were best.
I will go back, and I will find again
The ancient haunts of gods and hero-men,
Take counsel of the Delphian oracle,
Learn how to make life wise and beautiful."
You know the places, Athens, Astolat,
Carthage and Ulster, Troy and Camelot.
But you were with me like a clinging ghost;
Seeking more worthy loves, I loved you most.
Yours was the will I did, in singing chains,
Yours the consuming fever in my veins.
Far off and underneath enchanted moons,
My feet kept pace to your impetuous tunes.
Be friend to me a little; for the rest,
Withhold your trust from one who has confessed
A thousand nights of infidelities;
But I am done with sailing shadowed seas,
And am come home with breast torn wide apart,
To press my heart against your furious heart.

                                    Helene Mullins

3

Encore Une Fois

What shall I write that has not been written,
What may one say that has not been said
By Greek, Egyptian, by painted Briton,
  By men long dead?

Indian poets, Chinese, and Persian,
Have they not noted that life is brief,
That the green leaf turns by a sad perversion
  A yellow leaf?

Some Turk or Tartar, Roumanian, Roman
(A safe assumption), sang long ago
That all the good songs have been sung—and no man
  Exclaimed: *"No, no!"*

But nevertheless, though the thought's distressing,
In the year three thousand some silver tongue
Will re-express what I'm now expressing—
  And live unhung!

Lee Wilson Dodd

How Brief a Thing

The time being winter, now, the breath
Is visibly a little frost
That ventures on the empty air
And scatters and is lost.

And galleries of timeless stars
And hills that stand outside of death
Lean down across the dark to learn
How brief a thing is breath.

David Morton

For R. C. B.

Life comes a-hurrying,
  Or life lags slow;
But you've stopped worrying—
  Let it go!
Some call it gloomy,
  Some call it jake;
They're very little to me—
  Let them eat cake!
Some find it fair,
  Some think it hooey,
Many people care;
  But we don't, do we?

Dorothy Parker

Marble-Top

At counters where I eat my lunch
  In dim arcades of industry,
I cock my elbows up and munch
  Whatever food occurs to me.

By many mirrors multiplied
  My silly face is not exalted;
And when I leave I have inside
  An egg-and-lettuce and a malted.

And just to hear the pretty peal
  Of merry maids at their pimento
Is more to me than any meal
  Or banquet that I ever went to.

E. B. White

5

Song

My heart leaps up when I behold
A rainbow in the sky;
Contrariwise, my blood runs cold
When little boys go by.
For little boys as little boys
No special hate I carry,
But now and then they grow to men,
And when they do, they marry.
No matter how they tarry,
Eventually they marry.
And, swine among the pearls,
They marry little girls.

Oh, somewhere, somewhere an infant plays
With parents who feed and clothe him.
Their lips are sticky with pride and praise,
But I have begun to loathe him.
Yes, I loathe with a loathing shameless
This child who to me is nameless.
This bachelor child
   in his carriage
Gives never a thought to marriage,
But a person can hardly say "knife"
Before he demands a wife.

I never see an infant (male),
A-sleeping in the sun,
Without I turn a trifle pale
And think: Is *he* the one?
Oh, first he'll want to crop his curls,
And then he'll want a pony,
And then he'll think of pretty girls

6

And holy matrimony.
This Walker-Gordon crony
Will sigh for matrimony.
A cat without a mouse
Is he without a spouse.

Oh, somewhere he bubbles bubbles of milk
And quietly sucks his thumbs.
His cheeks are roses painted on silk,
And his teeth are tucked in his gums.
But, alas, the teeth will begin to grow
And the bubbles will cease to bubble;
Given a score of years or so,
The roses will turn to stubble.
He'll sell a bond, or he'll write a book,
And his eyes will get that acquisitive look,
And raging and ravenous for the kill,
He'll boldly ask for the hand of Jill.
This infant whose middle
Is diapered still
Will want to marry
My daughter Jill.

Oh, sweet be his slumber and moist his middle;
My dreams, I fear, are infanticiddle.
A fig for embryo Lohengrins!
I'll open all of his safety pins,
I'll pepper his powder, and salt his bottle,
And give him readings from Aristotle.
Sand for his spinach I'll gladly bring,
And tabasco sauce for his teething ring,
And an elegant, elegant alligator
To play with in the perambulator.
Then perhaps he'll struggle through fire and water
To marry somebody else's daughter.

                                    Ogden Nash

Ordeal by Family

I've been out where the Blues begin,
Stopping at home with my kith and kin,
Where the handclasp's firm, and the smile is humorous,
And Family Friends are a bit too numerous.

Oh, Family Friends are staunch and sound
　　Their virtues all are double.
Family Friends, they rally round
　　Whenever you're in trouble.
Family Friends are worth their weight
　　In any goods you carry.
But they incline to speculate
　　On when you're going to marry.

Family Friends, if they're feminine,
Wear their chins in a triple line.
Or, if of masculine gender, they
Have positive views on the NRA.

Oh, Family Friends will fight for you
　　To the utmost ditch.
Family Friends are loyal and true,
　　Sometimes even rich.
But Family Friends are apt to fret
　　About your squandered wages.
And lest you haply might forget,
　　They always mention ages.

Oh, Family Friends sit round in a ring
And give you counsel on everything.
They think red nails are an incongruity.
They urge you to buy a good annuity.
Their smiles are kind and their eyes are mild.
They want to fatten you up, poor child,

And feed you lovely chicken-and-waffley
Meals designed to upset you awfully.
They say "How tragic!" and "What a pity!'
And of your life in the fervid city
They ask in an interested kind of way
But never listen to what you say.

Oh, Family Friends are noble folk,
   With noble views on life.
Each husband tells his little joke,
   Applauded by his wife.
All the men are gentlemen,
   The ladies more than such.
And now that I'm away again,
   I miss them very much.

Phyllis McGinley

Song for Snow

The earth is lighter
Than the sky,
The world is wider
Than in spring.
Along white roads
The sleighs go by,
Icily sweet
The sleighbells ring.

The birds are gone
Into the South,
The leaves are fallen
To the ground,
But singing shakes
Each sleighbell's mouth
And leaf-like ears
Turn to the sound.

Elizabeth Coatsworth

Uncalled-for Epitaph

G. MC N.

"Oh boy! I'm down—I'm up—in Heaven!—
"The Nine Apostles—No, it's Seven!—
"Oh boy! St. Peter's got the ball!—
"I'm wrong, it's Luke—No, wait, it's Paul!—"
Good old Graham!
Always the saham.

Ogden Nash

Those Who Read in Bed

There are no late-hour devotees
  As irreproachable as these,
Who sink to rest in pillowed nooks
  And stick their ostrich heads in books.

Dim astigmatic votaries
  Care not for crackers spread with cheese.
They read, while duller folk explore
  Within the open ice-chest door.

All worldly pleasures call in vain;
  They lead the night life of the brain
And take their festive midnight snack
  From volumes bound in red or black.

There are no late-hour devotees
  As calmly ravenous as these,
Who dine like predatory birds
  On little dark exciting words.

Persis Greely Anderson

Le Jaseroque

[THE JABBERWOCK]

Il brilgue: les tôves lubricilleux
Se gyrent en vrillant dans le guave,
Enmîmés sont les gougebosqueux,
Et le mômerade horsgrave.

Garde-toi du Jaseroque, mon fils!
La gueule qui mord; la griffe qui prend!
Garde-toi de l'oiseau Jube, évite
Le frumieux Band-à-prend.

Son glaive vorpal en main il va-
T-à la recherche du fauve manscant;
Puis arrivé à l'arbre Té-Té,
Il y reste, réfléchissant.

Pendant qu'il pense, tout uffusé,
Le Jaseroque, à l'œil flambant,
Vient siblant par le bois tullegeais,
Et burbule en venant.

Un deux, un deux, par le milieu,
Le glaive vorpal fait pat-à-pan!
La bête défaite, avec sa tête,
Il rentre gallomphant.

As-tu tué le Jaseroque?
Viens à mon cœur, fils rayonnois!
O jour frabbegeais! Calleau! Callai!
Il cortule dans sa joie.

Il brilgue: les tôves lubricilleux
Se gyrent en vrillant dans le guave,
Enmîmés sont les gougebosqueux,
Et le mômerade horsgrave.

                              Frank L. Warrin, Jr.

11

God Saves the King (and Queen)

While the guard was being changed, an aeroplane a few feet above the roof narrowly averted striking Buckingham Palace. This caused the King and Queen, who were within, to make enquiries.—*Associated Press Bulletin.*

The guard were splendid red and gold,
The guard were six feet two and bold,
But the Royal Roof by a plane was grazed
And even the stalwart guard were dazed.
Said they to the airman, "Hey!"

The Queen in her lofty room was sitting,
Busy with all her worthy knitting,
And the King in his royal book was pasting
A bright new stamp there was no use wasting.
Said he to the Queen then, "See?"

Near to the roof the airman dipped.
"The royal chimneys may be clipped.
He's going to crash in the palace yard,
Or the Queen's own suite," cried the frightened guard.
Roared they to the airman, "Mind!"

"What," said the Queen, "is that distant humming?"
"I fear, my dear, it's defective plumbing,
We must get a crew to look at the drains.
Have they been fixed since the Tudor reigns?"
Said the Queen to the King then, "Eh?"

And now on high was a wilder roar;
The madcap ship would swoop, then soar.
"I fear it is hardly dignified;
Yet let us enquire what's wrong outside."
Said the Queen to the King then, "My!"

"Thank God you live and the crisis past;
The plane is down in Hyde Park at last."
The equerry bowed and then withdrew.
"I was just a little alarmed, weren't you?"
Said the Queen to her consort, "What!"

The King took a stamp from Timbuctoo
And pasted it there, page forty-two.
"Never allow a thing like noise
Ever to ruffle your royal poise,"
Said the King to his consort, "Pooh!"

Henrietta Fort Holland

Sea-Chill

When Mrs. John Masefield and her husband, the author of "I Must Go Down to the Seas Again," arrived here on a liner, she said to a reporter, "It was too uppy-downy, and Mr. Masefield was ill."—*News Item.*

I must go down to the seas again, where the billows romp and
    reel,
So all I ask is a large ship that rides on an even keel,
And a mild breeze and a broad deck with a slight list to leeward,
And a clean chair in a snug nook and a nice, kind steward.

I must go down to the seas again, the sport of wind and tide,
As the gray wave and the green wave play leapfrog over the side.
And all I want is a glassy calm with a bone-dry scupper,
A good book and a warm rug and a light, plain supper.

I must go down to the seas again, though there I'm a total loss,
And can't say which is worst, the pitch, the plunge, the roll,
    the toss.
But all I ask is a safe retreat in a bar well tended,
And a soft berth and a smooth course till the long trip's ended.

Arthur Guiterman

13

Invocation

Smoot plans tariff ban on improper books.—*News Item.*

Senator Smoot (Republican, Ut.)
Is planning a ban on smut.
Oh rooti-ti-toot for Smoot of Ut.
And his reverend occiput.
Smite, Smoot, smite for Ut.,
Grit your molars and do your dut.,
Gird up your l—ns,
Smite h–p and th–gh,
We'll all be Kansas
By and by.

Smite, Smoot, for the Watch and Ward,
For Hiram Johnson and Henry Ford,
For Bishop Cannon and John D., Junior,
For ex-Gov. Pinchot of Pennsylvunia,
For John S. Sumner and Elder Hays
And possibly Edward L. Bernays,
For Orville Poland and Ella Boole,
For Mother Machree and the Shelton pool.
When smut's to be smitten
Smoot will smite
For G–d, for country,
And Fahrenheit.

Senator Smoot is an institute
Not to be bribed with pelf;
He guards our homes from erotic tomes
By reading them all himself.
Smite, Smoot, smite for Ut.,
They're smuggling smut from Balt. to Butte!
Strongest and sternest
Of your s–x
Scatter the scoundrels
From Can. to Mex.!

14

Smite, Smoot, for Smedley Butler,
For any good man by the name of Cutler,
Smite for the W.C.T.U.,
For Rockne's team and for Leader's crew,
For Florence Coolidge and Admiral Byrd,
For Billy Sunday and John D., Third,
For Grantland Rice and for Albie Booth,
For the Woman's Auxiliary of Duluth,
Smite, Smoot,
Be rugged and rough,
Smut if smitten
Is front-page stuff.

Ogden Nash

Horned Owl

The north horned owl
Has lanterns in his head;
His is the poet's soul
When all is said:
Stars like cold stones brim
A cobalt bowl;
He sits upon the rim,
His gold eyes roll.

He deals out death more fine
Than your philosophy;
His pulpit a blue pine,
His text a tree;
The mouse that spurts below
Approves by three
Red pinpricks in the snow
That silver accuracy.

Joseph Auslander

15

Elegies for a Passing World

RIVERTON

Here am I among elms again—ah, look
How, high above low windows hung with white.
Dark on white dwellings, rooted among rock,
They rise like iron ribs that pillar night!
The stars are high again; the night is clear;
The bed rolls with the old uneven floor;
The air is still again—I lie and hear
The river always falling at the door.

—O elms! O river! aid me at this turn—
Their passing makes my late imperative:
They flicker now who frightfully did burn,
And I must tell their beauty while I live.
Changing their grace as water in its flight,
And gone like water; give me then the art,
Firm as night-frozen ice found silver-bright,
That holds the splendor though the days depart.

A HOUSE OF THE EIGHTIES

No more as once in dreams it draws me there,
All fungus-grown and sunken in damp ground—
No more as once when waking I gazed down
On elms like water weeds in moonlit air
Or heard the August downpour with its dull full sound—
Drenched hedges and the hillside and the night,
The largest house in sight—
And thought it sunken out of time or drowned
As hulks in Newark Bay are soaked and slowly drown.

—The ugly stained-glass window on the stair,
Dark-panelled dining-room, the guinea fowls' fierce clack,
The great gray cat that on the oven slept—
My father's study with its books and birds,
His scornful tone, his eighteenth-century words,

16

His green door sealed with baize
—Today I travel back
To find again that one fixed point he kept
And left me for the day
In which this other world of theirs grows dank, decays
And founders and goes down.

Edmund Wilson

Unfinished History

We have loved each other in this time twenty years
And with such love as few men have in them even for
One or for the marriage month or the hearing of

Three nights' carts in the street but it will leave them:
We have been lovers the twentieth year now:
Our bed has been made in many houses and evenings:

The apple-tree moves at the window in this house:
There were palms rattled the night through in one:
In one there were red tiles and the sea's hours:

We have made our bed in the changes of many months—and the
Light of the day is still overlong in the windows
Till night shall bring us the lamp and one another:

Those that have seen her have no thought what she is:
Her face is clear in the sun as a palmful of water:
Only by night and in love are the dark winds on it. . .

I wrote this poem that day when I thought
Since we have loved we two so long together
Shall we have done together—all love gone?

Or how then will it change with us when the breath
Is no more able for such joy and the blood is
Thin in the throat and the time not come for death?

Archibald MacLeish

Eschatology

I have no care for Systematic Theology,
But oh, the recurrent hour of bile that brings
Fainness for specialization in Eschatology
(Greek, you recall, for study of all Last Things!).

Come, day when the wealth of the world is less than tuppence,
The seas unfretted, and the monuments down,
When the proud have got their ultimate come-uppance,
And on the seventh New York the sand lies brown;

And all my sloth and failure, all my passion
One with the sorrows of the Gaul and Goth,
And all our fireproof homes are burnt and ashen,
And in the moth-proof closet dwells the moth;

And every most unspeakable thing is spoken,
And rust is in the unrusting pipes of brass,
And all unbreakable things at last are broken,
Shatter'd the non-shatterable glass.

Morris Bishop

Ego

She is an island
in the ocean
off the coast.
On a bright day
she sees at most
the tint of trees,
the line of spray
in misty motion;
on a dark night,
the lighted highland.

Upon occasion
she believes
she catches sight
of people, sees
some of her kind
upon the *plage*.
Her eye deceives—
a mere evasion
of the mind—
just a mirage.

Peggy Bacon

The Game

'Hide' was the word, for most of us were hiders,
'And Seek' began by warning with a shout.
Attics and barns and trees were best providers:
In some of them they never found us out.

Count to five hundred: Five, ten, fifteen, twen'y
(To be the last one home is half the game)
Till the slow shadows find the dwindling many
Cheating the supper bell of prior claim.

Out of our time, O strict exiguous memory,
What have we sought and, seeking, failed or found,
Which in the instrument of simple summary
Excels the love of old enchanted ground?

The ingle, nook, and hour all have vanished,
The hidden and the hider, done and by;
But in the child runs still the sweet unbanished
'You're it,' 'Five hundred,' 'Coming, coming,' I cry!

David McCord

Hospital Song

[COMPOSED WHILE EMERGING FROM THE ETHER]

Hospitals simply enchant me.
    I'm a hard-bitten hospital fan.
I dote on the service they grant me
    And their resolute rescue of Man.
Oh, I warble a hey-diddle-diddle
    In honest and garrulous praise
For the beds that rise up in the middle
    And the girls that come down with the trays;
For the gown that you wear
    And the days that are spent
In the rubber-tired chair
    And the oxygen tent;
For the pulse that they take
    When you're cross or you're flustered;
For Barium shake
    And ubiquitous custard.
Yes, hark while I carol a resonant air
To hospital treatment and hospital fare!

BUT

I don't like my breakfast at seven in the morning.
Why do they *have* to wake you with the shadows on the lawn?
Oh, I ken John Peel
May have liked an early meal,
But I *don't* want my porridge at breaking of the dawn.

How dear to my heart are the faces
    That visitors wear when they call;
The nurse Who Likes Interesting Cases,
    And the chart that she hides in the hall;
The beautiful way that your skin turns

All pallid, poetic, and white;
The quaintly susceptible internes,
    And the married ones given to flight;
The broth that you sup
    And the milk that you snub;
The spoon in the cup
    And the alcohol rub;
The flowers you get,
    And the head surgeon's joke;
And the lone cigarette
    They allow you to smoke.
Yes, I sing to the heavens, I chant to the breeze
Of hospital diets and hospital fees.

BUT

I don't like the mattresses that corrugate your backbone.
And I don't want assistance when I wield a brush and comb.
Oh, hospitals are nice,
As I've mentioned once or twice,
But—lean a little closer—*I would rather be at home.*

                                    Phyllis McGinley

Song for Thrift Week

            As soon
            As a squirrel
            Has gathered
            Its bin full,
            A hunter
            Stands ready
            To pepper
            Its skin full.
                Mildred Weston

Farewell Voyaging World!

It was the departure, the sun was risen,
the light came across the flat sea, the yellow blades
fell like swords on the small white houses
the half hoisted sail creaked on the ship
the seagulls hovered in circles and cried
on the foredeck the sailors stood at the capstan

the moving light made the land look as if it were moving
the houses shifted the windows changed
cocks crew and the hens strutted into the street
and you went down the path of shells, carrying
a box on your shoulder a bundle in your hand
I followed hearing ahead the sound of your feet

but you carried also the invisible
you carried also the unspoken
what we could not say what we had not said
what we had not lived and could never live
what we had lived but could not be forgotten
where will you remember it where again will you sit down

at a little foreign table reading a paper
the news a month old and our hearts a month dead
with a strange clock above you and a bird in a cage
chirping in another language
but not yet now it is still the daybreak
look they are hoisting the sail and singing

the moving light makes the land seem to move
it is we who are going away and not you
we take away with us an indecipherable heritage
time is broken in our hands
it is we who leave you here in a motionless ship
as we begin the immeasurable circle

say goodbye to us make your farewells
the earth is leaving you the earth is going
never again shall we come to this permanent ship
or you everlasting with your box on your shoulder
it will always be daybreak with us, the beginning,
we shall never be older or wiser or dead.

Conrad Aiken

How It Might Have Appeared

IF (1) LEUCONOË HAD CONSULTED MAE WEST INSTEAD OF Q. H.
FLACCUS AND (2) DOROTHY PARKER HAD BEEN MAE'S GHOST WRITER

"Tu ne quaesieris, scire nefas . . ."—(Horace: Book I, Ode XI)

Why all this awful stew about
    How long you've got to live?
There's nothing you can do about
    It—give, girl, give!

For life comes hot and hurrying
    Till zip!—and you are dead!
So what's the good of worrying
    Your dumb, blonde head?

Oh, better to be snatching at
    The boons of board and bed
Than sit around a-scratching at
    Your blonde, dumb head!

And better to be sinning in
    A gown of silk and satin
Than sit around a-chinning in
    This goddam Latin!

Morrie Ryskind

23

A Fairly Sad Story

I think that I shall never know
Why I am thus, and I am so.
Around me, other girls inspire
In men the swing and sweep of fire,
The cooling clarity of glass,
The tenderness of April grass,
The durability of granite—
But me! I know not how to plan it.
What guys I've met in Cupid's deadlock
Were—shall we say?—born out of wedlock.
They broke my heart, they stilled my song,
And said they had to run along,
Explaining, so to sop my tears,
First came their parents or careers.
But do you think experience
Has lent me wisdom, calm, and sense?
Alas! In matters such as these
I'll never know my groceries.
Though she's a fool who seeks to capture
The twenty-first fine careless rapture,
I must go on, till ends my rope,
Who from my birth was cursed with hope.
A heart in half is chaste, archaic;
But mine resembles a mosaic.
The thing's become ridiculous!
Why am I so, why am I thus?

Dorothy Parker

Post-Graduate

Hope it was that tutored me,
    And Love that taught me more;
And now I learn at Sorrow's knee
    The self-same lore.

Dorothy Parker

24

Ode for an Epoch

When at our history men stand amazed,
When there is light to see
The nature of such things as are to be,
And shall be—then—
When some, our captains, may have grown as quaint
And crazed as any mediaeval saint
To marveling eyes of a new order of men . . .

When all that so involves our baffled day
Is passed away,
And these our cities, like Carthage or like Tyre,
Grow strange with alien arrogance and power,
That seemed the unfolding flower
And deepest utterance of Mankind's desire . . .

When our concerns, our tyrannous machines
That were the means
To no sure end, but turned against their masters—
Our intricate finance that would not fit
For all our wit
In any pattern save foretold disaster's—
When all these singular things,
Even our wings
That hummed and drummed, a locust-cloud, through heaven,
Are gathered to the ingurgitating past,
And men at last, steadfast
In flesh and blood, are for new sins forgiven . . .

Then even the Jeremiahs of our time,
Or those whose minds can climb
The clear, cold air of reason, or those others
Of hot head and hot heart—
Inveighing, for their part,
In the belief that all men may be brothers—
Even the words of these

Like leaves from autumn trees
May flutter to dust, or start mere bright surprise
Mixed, it may be, with laughter,
In minds that, after
An age, confute our cleverest surmise—
Mixed, it may be, with sighs
To think that on this wise
Our world-in-space, incredible to Time
For its swift power to move,
Crawls slower in the groove
Of progress than a snail its trail of slime . . .

Then the historian
Poring upon some plan
He draughts, with dates, with gazetteer and chart,
And burnishing fine prose
To explicate our woes,
Though still confounded by the human heart,
Will with a sage disdain
Make our confusion plain,
Precisely point the errors of all schools,
And, through the zodiac,
Show on a crazy tack
Our barque of souls, our precious ship of fools . . .

Meanwhile, the wintry tree
Cased in glare ice will be
A palace of blossom to the soft south air;
Meanwhile, rivers run
Under moon, under sun;
Mountains their flamboyant sunsets wear;
And deserts lie as still
As fields that men may till,
And stars to wondering lovers sparkle near,
Though far, cold worlds of light
To aging sight—
And poets are drunken with the atmosphere . . .

And rhythms fall and rise
In the earth, in the skies,
And fugitive, fortunate moments stand alway;
And men contrive a god
From cloud or clod;
And night we know . . . and day . . .

Meanwhile, the hurried blood
Whirls us through myriad mood,
And instants are immortal in our breath,
And deeds are blowing grain,
And love we know, and pain . . .
And life . . . and death . . .

William Rose Benét

The Escape

Going from us at last,
He gave himself forever
Unto the mudded nest,
Unto the dog and the beaver.

Sick of the way we stood,
He pondered upon flying,
Or envied the triple thud
Of horses' hooves; whose neighing

Came to him sweeter than talk,
Whereof he too was tired.
No silences now he broke,
No emptiness explored.

Going from us, he never
Sent one syllable home.
We called him wild; but the plover
Watched him, and was tame.

Mark Van Doren

The Party

Come, Arabella, fetch the cake,
On a dish with silver handles.
Oh, mercy! Feel the table shake!
Lucinda, light the candles.

    For Mr. Migg is thir-ty,
    Is thir–ty,
    Is thir—ty,
    The years are crawling over him
    Like wee red ants.
    Oh, three times ten is thir-ty,
    Is for–ty,
    Is fif—ty,
    The further off from England
    The nearer is to France.

The little flames they bob and jig,
The dining hall is breezy.
Quick! Puff your candles, Mr. Migg,
The little flames die easy.

    For Mr. Migg is for-ty,
    Is for–ty,
    Is for—ty,
    The years are crawling over him
    Like wee red ants.
    Oh, four times ten is for-ty,
    Is fif–ty,
    Is six—ty,
    And creeping through the icing,
    The other years advance.

Why, Arabella, here's a ring!
Lucinda, here's a thimble!

For Mr. Migg there's not a thing—
'Tis not, I trust, a symbol!

For Mr. Migg is fif-ty,
Is fif–ty,
Is fif—ty,
The years are crawling over him
Like wee red ants.
Oh, five times ten is fif-ty,
Is six–ty,
Is seven—ty.
Lucinda, take the cake away,
We're going to the dance.

Ogden Nash

Snow

Softly, softly through the snow
My thoughts go,
Leaving no print and no sound
Above sleeping ground,

Quietly moving across the road there
Lightly as prayer,
Skimming the fields in the blue twilight
Lying white,

Touching the trees rising black and still,
Curving the hill—
Beyond this drifted whiteness trying to find
The living mind,

Behind this frozen moment trying to trace
Love on a lost face;
Gently, desperately, like fingers of the blind,
Trying to find.

Virginia Woods Bellamy

Heroica

Green laurel withers on the head
  And golden weighs it down:
Tell me, all you heroic dead,
  Is there a happy crown?

                    Marya Mannes

II. FEBRUARY: *The fountain is dry at the Plaza*

The Formal Dinner

It was a formal dinner. 'Neath the gleam
  Of mellow candlelight the napery shone,
  Crimsoning where the lavish rose was strown.
Vague shapes of waiters drifted in a dream.
And gaiety came to cast its silken spell
  Over the men, in sober whites and blacks,
  Over the ladies' pink lascivious backs.
God! I love mussels *à la Béchamel!*
    Ha! ha! ha!
    Tra! la! la!
    Ça c'est bon pour l'estomac!

It was a formal dinner. In their holders
  Nuts posed like odalisques. And mirth waxed high,
  Tributes were paid to many a laughing eye,
And indiscretions breathed o'er pearly shoulders.
And the proud hostess, queening o'er us all,
  Bowed like a lily to her *vis-à-vis;*
  And we had *côtelettes de veau farcies,*
And *champignons,* ay, *à la provençale!*
    Ha! ha! ha!
    Tra! la! la!
    Ça c'est bon pour l'estomac!

Only an hour the rose of joy may bloom,
  Only an hour; the quiet blossom closes.
  The hostess, meaninglessly arch, proposes:
"Shall we not pass into the drawing-room?"
Ah, do not speak. A peaceful warm constriction
  Lingers; a far faint thought of *artichauts,*
  A clearer sense of *beignets d'abricots,*
And Benedictine for our benediction.
    Ha! ha! ha!
    Tra! la! la!
    Ça c'est bon pour l'estomac!
                          Morris Bishop

What a Young Woman of Eighteen Should Know

Young ladies who read erudite books in the subway
    Really shouldn't do it.
It is a very dangerous type of pastime,
    If they but knew it.

I knew a girl named Elizabeth Mc*Something*—
    A literato—
Who got on a downtown local at Columbus Circle
    With a volume of Plato.

When she looked up whose eye should she encounter
    But an old satyr's.
He was wearing a sort of dirty familiar smile
    And a pair of gaiters.

Before she could jump from the window or call a policeman
    Or hurl a tomato,
He leaned over and very knowingly murmured:
    "I see you read Plato!"

Well, Elizabeth sat there and didn't know what to do.
    Something told her
That if she didn't get her wits collected and put him in his place
    He'd get bolder.

The old goat (she found out later that he taught at Columbia
    In the summer season)
Opened his briefcase without Aye, Yes, or No and offered her
    "The Critique of Pure Reason."

Friends later told her she should have taken it,
    Snubbed him, and kept it.
But she had been reared to value honor. She felt
    She couldn't accept it.

The psychoanalyst traced all her troubles to that incident.
  She never outgrew it.
Girls who read Plato in subways are playing with fire.
  They shouldn't do it.

Jake Falstaff

Pensive Thoughts on Infant Prodigies

Young Bach copied music by moonlight
  When merely a lad of eleven,
And Haydn could sing almost any hard thing
  Before he was six or was seven.

At a concert of London's elect
  Young Mozart—or so I've been told—
Played his own overture, and I'm perfectly sure
  The tickets were easily sold.

Chopin was so brilliant and winsome,
  So charming, so tender of years,
His improvisations were quite the sensations
  Of people with musical ears.

Beethoven, adorable baby,
  When still very chubby and fat,
Sent his nursemaid away and devoted the day
  To writing a thing in E flat.

Yet no matter how often I read
  Of babies whose childhood was fiery,
I cannot hit G at the same time as C
  Without getting hot and perspiry.

Mariana Bonnell Davenport

Relic

A darky dank
as the black mud
of a river bank
after a flood—
ebon god
of a cult evil,
totem odd
of a tribe primeval,
jungle male
of an ancient era,
before Baal,
before Hera—
curves his back
and heaves a shovel;
sleek and black,
he bends to grovel,
working down
in an excavation,
in a new town,
in a young nation.

They blast the rock
and raise the glories
of a city block
a hundred stories;
the artifact
and the fine appliance
are made exact
to a modern science—
held and linked
with a latter passion;
on a world extinct,
a world to fashion.

Peggy Bacon

Apostrophe to a Flea

Nimble and unresting flea,
Do not leap away from me!

Though somewhat different in kind,
We are of a similar mind.

Like yourself, O agile flea,
I hop and skip incessantly

From arid here to barren there,
Leaving a zigzag track of air.

Like yourself, I skip and jump
From Life's head to Life's rump,

Scarcely knowing which is which.
I am the flea, the bite, the itch.

Oh, what a destiny we've missed!—
Each a great Industrialist

Leaping with harmonious mind
Upon the earth's immense behind,

The while she sleeps her ancient sleep
And grazes apathetic sheep.

Sometimes in quietness I seem
To hear her scratching in a dream,

With fingers of cool wind and sea,
The bites of multitudinous me—
Her Super-Flea.

O Lesser Insect, you are bound
By lack of Science to the ground.

But we from singing spires shall leap
In aëroplanes upon the deep,

Attack the sylphs who linger there
In the last coverts of the air,

Till they run howling through the blue
And we in roaring swarms pursue.

O Flea, behold us overrun
The purlieus of the shaken sun

And hop and skip and jump and bite
Between the mountains and the light.

The backward aether shall be taught
How sales resistance may be fought,

And mass production shall resound
Tormented leagues above the ground.

The gullies of the moon shall bloom
With a new industrial boom,

And Einstein's void be further bent
To lines of eight and ten per cent.

Oh, what flea-orbits we shall trace
Upon the Universal Face,

While mighty Bankers organize
The vast resources of the skies—

Munition factories in Mars
And tariff rings around the stars.

O, nimble and prolific flea,
Lie down and meditate with me
Our slightly different in degree
But common destiny!

Samuel Hoffenstein

Ennui

Sweethearts drowned inside the shuttle
In a manner strangely subtle,
Bits of former lion trainers
Neatly packed in jade containers,
Over-stubborn aged sires
Cut in two with piano wires,
Opera stars with precious voices
Found dismembered in Rolls-Royces,
Several bankers newly mated
Suddenly asphyxiated.
In the pure unsullied air,
Central Park or Union Square,
Bodies of some high officials
Branded with their own initials,
Several undeserving blighters
Burned to death with Dunhill lighters,
Lovers pushed from lofty girders,
Rich dame victim of sheepherders. . . .

. . . . . *Let's have more Artistic Murders.*

Parke Cummings

On St. Valentine's Day

Madame is tender with M'sieu,
The staircase Cupid thumbs his nose,
And Higgins, taking breakfast up,
Pinches the housemaid as he goes.

Irma Brandeis

Catch Old St. Valentine By the Toe

St. Valentine's day is a February day,
St. Patrick's falls in March;
St. Swithin's day votes yea or nay
On whether we drip or parch.
St. Patrick trod the Irish sod,
By choice, if not by birth,
And I'm unaware of exactly where
St. Swithin walked the earth.
But Valentine, St. Valentine,
I trust he trod on a porcupine.

The Doctor Ditmars of his day
Is a phrase that applies to Patrick;
An efficient saint in his chosen way,
Though perhaps a mite theatric.
St. Swithin did I know not what,
But piecing the bits together,
I suppose his claim to immortal fame
Had something to do with weather.
But Valentine became the patron
Of the maid who'd rather be a matron.

St. Patrick's day is brave and bold,
With the music blaring gaily,
With buckles and braid and a big parade,
And shamrock and shillelagh.
St. Swithin's day is a splendid day
And I'm glad that the day is his,
Though every year, I regret to say,
I forget which day it is.
But Valentine, St. Valentine,
His day is over-endocrine.

St. Valentine's day is a Broadway day,
A day of reeking loves,

When they stuff the marts with bleeding hearts
And goddamned twittering doves.
O crooner's day, O swooner's day,
O day of versicles vile!
O day of the smile in every tear,
And the tear in every smile!
Marshmallow whip and mailing lists!
Meringue of exhibitionists!

Then be my angel, dearest dear,
My darling and my poppet,
My gambolling lamb, my ham what am,
My priceless Persian coppet.
Be my gazelle, my wishing well,
My sacred garden spot,
My *raison d'être,* etc., etc.,
But never my you-know-what.
Be everything, my love, that's mine,
But not if I know it, my Valentine.

Ogden Nash

New Ice

Children, swallow swift, go by
Purple cheeked and collared high,
Coated smartly, coated quaintly.
In the new ice mirrored faintly,
Scarves of scarlet, caps of green,
Sweaters gaudy and serene,
Black's prevailing sombre hue
Turned in sunshine mussel-blue,
Whirl about or stiffly grope
Like one vast kaleidoscope.

None should need to summon twice
Ice-blue steel to steel-blue ice.

Olive Ward

41

Seven Nuns Watch an Express Train

Seven nuns in dusty black
Stood beside the railroad track.
Huddled stood like seven sheep
Newly wakened out of sleep;
Dazed with motion, drenched with sound,
Flinched and bobbed but stood their ground,
Shoulders twitching, flickering eyes . . .

Then slept again, remote and wise.

Eunice Tietjens

Intimations at Fifty-eighth Street

The fountain is dry at the Plaza,
   The sycamore trees go bare;
The ivy is sere and it has a
   Resigned and immutable air.

The lady is cold in the fountain,
   The sitter is cold on the ledge,
The Plaza is gaunt as a mountain,
   The air is a knife with an edge.

But what is this sniff and this twitter,
   And what is the pluck at my vest?
What gleam in the eye of the sitter?
   What lamb of a cloud in the west?

The earth is but held in solution,
   And March will release before long
The lady in brazen ablution,
   The trees and the fountain in song!

E. B. White

Episode of the Cherry Tree

An ill-advised
And foolish thing,
For us to harp
Upon this string;
The world will think
We're puzzled by
A patriot
Who would not lie.

Mildred Weston

From St. Luke's

Under the knife
as he looked back
he saw life
through a bright crack
saw movement
through a door ajar
heard voices
from afar;
much he hankered
to live again
but was anchored
to an icy pain;
in a little time
he would be dead
white as lime
dull as lead,
nothing ahead
but this one moment
—this cold black
perpetual moment.

Peggy Bacon

43

Peregrine's Sunday Song

When I have grown foolish
And ripe for my grave,
O, I'll be a mulish
And stubborn old knave!

I'll open my coffer
That's gilt and engraved;
Only those who suffer
Shall share what I've saved.

I'll build a great castle
In the heart of the town,
Like a long golden tassel
The clouds have let down.

I'll spread a broad table
Where thieves may repair;
There'll be oats in my stable
For the murderer's mare.

Most brightly on one day
My lamp shall be lit,
And Sunday, Sunday,
Is the sad name of it.

For then to the churches
The gentlefolk come,
But the sinner searches
Bare streets for a crumb;

O, bare but for sparrows,
And these eating dung!
On his breast-bone his sorrows
Like mill-stones are hung.

The saved and the shriven
Have consecrate meat,
But the poor unforgiven
Get nothing to eat.

While bells from the steeple
Rain silver on grief,
I'll call wicked people
To pudding and beef.

To plum-cake and liquor,
To sugary buns;
O, I shall call quicker
The wickeder ones!

If my hand should be hostile
To these hungry friends
I'll climb fire and frost till
My pilgrimage ends.

If I held me their better
By the very least part
Of a hair, 'twere a fetter
That rusted my heart.

O, few merry-makers
Will come to my board;
No salt in the shakers
I'll need to afford.

Much weeping will season
The viands with salt,
But I'll give none a reason
To grieve for his fault.

Eve shall not eat apples
Nor Cain wheaten bread
While something yet dapples
His white hand with red.

His thanks none shall owe me
Save for courtesy's sake;
I'll let the young Salome
Cut slices of cake,

Which she'll bring on a platter
To everyone,
For why should it matter
To me about John?

None shall be so rude as
To show pity or pride;
Broken-necked Judas
Shall sit by my side.

My tables and trestles
May fall down accursed,
But I'll have filled vessels
To charity first.

"How got you this jam?" ask
The prudenter sort;
"This silver and damask?
This pastry and port?"

"By murder? By arson?
By stabbing a knight?
By strangling a parson?"
Perhaps they are right.

Now I sing this fasting
By an elder tree;
Life everlasting
Is not for me.

I've leave to squander
What I never can keep,
However I wander
Or walk in my sleep.

Elinor Wylie

Form Was the World

The boy looked out of eyes like Euclid's eyes.
Form was the world. Precision of part to part
Was just and perfect. The flint's form, the penny's bright size,
Troubled the nerves with knowledge of pure art.

The grooving of separate things together,
Perception of arched, waved, round,
Was more than the pride of blue weather.
The turn of the wheel to the ground

Or the curl of a dropped apple rind
Struck home as much joy and wonder
As the high walk of the wind,
As the roll and flow of thunder.

I remember it thinly now . . .
                    Brain's weariness is mine
Because, spontaneous, I no longer feel
My breath caught up at the strict and valid line,
Or stare at the right rondure of the wheel.

Maurice English

Let Earth Go Whirling

All the simple things that brain takes heart to task for
Lie on the heart unhappy and unsolved.
The poor, hurt heart that knows not what to ask for
Still asks to know why the earth last revolved.

Was it for wit, that saved men from themselves?
Was it for law, that wit devised for reason?
Was it for time, whose hours go down by twelves?
Was it to leave behind the love whose light is treason?

Breath, that blood can better; food, drink, that better blood,
Bind, as earth round roots, around the brain's shrewd centres.
Earth saves no tree from evil, blood makes no wisdom good,
It is the heart alone, the deep heart, that life enters.

O heart, let earth go whirling, and never wonder why.
Motion can teach but little to the breast that holds your grief.
The tree that stands most rooted is the tree least like to die.
Cling to your flesh and bone, O heart, and bear your bitter leaf.

Raymond Holden

Fable with No Moral

There was a most persuasive writer, I am told,
Who, with a difference, had the Midas touch:
Whatever stuff he wrote, the writing sold;
Good, bad, or bad, it did not matter much.
He was a yea-sayer of the deepest dye,
As clean and solid as a cake of soap.
He lathered well, and kept his income high;
In his bright lexicon no word like "Nope."

What people wanted said, he gladly said,
Because he also yearned to be well read.

48

"They will remember me when I am dead,"
He thought, but he was wrong. Not being clay,
But soap that lived by making lather pay,
He did not die. He washed himself away.

There was another writer, so I've heard,
Who, in his novels, tolled the sombre note.
He'd spend a week deciding on a word,
Yet barely sold the best of what he wrote.
A critic said, "Fit audience though few
Will like him if they like a story stark."
He read the critic twice, and took the cue:
His bite was much more deadly than his bark.

What people wanted filled him with disgust.
He was the kind no readers feel they must.
"They will remember me when I am dust,"
He cried, but he was wrong. It was no blow
To them; they let him come, and let him go,
And did not know. They simply did not know.

John Holmes

Fulfilment

For this my mother wrapped me warm,
And called me home against the storm,
And coaxed my infant nights to quiet,
And gave me roughage in my diet,
And tucked me in my bed at eight,
And clipped my hair, and marked my weight,
And watched me as I sat and stood:
That I might grow to womanhood
To hear a whistle, and drop my wits,
And break my heart to clattering bits.

Dorothy Parker

49

Prelude

Woman, woman, let us say these things to each other
as slowly as if we were mill-stones in a field
with centuries of rain in which to say them,
let us say in the morning
   "we do not hear each other"
and in the evening
   "we do not hear each other"
and let us be bewildered by the yes and no,
the plus and minus, the where and there,
the hour in the thistledown, the acre in the seed,

and walk distracted in the world of men,
bow to all voices,
see ourselves in the mirrors of all minds,
smile at all faces,
and in the beneficent evening, once more, always,
sleep in all peacefulness.

Conrad Aiken

Last Will

What shall we leave our children, you and I?
A sudden passion for a salty sky;
A love of villages beneath a hill
And low white houses that lie snug and still;
A thirst for freedom, and a restless mind,
A hungry seeking for what few may find;
Poor little wretches, with their mother's way
Of counting always on a Lucky Day.
Poor little wretches, whom their father gave
The silver fortune of a breaking wave.
And still, more fortunate than those, I guess,
Who have no heritage of happiness;
Who, with a golden spoon, lap up cream

But have no certainty of wish or dream;
Who have their Chippendale and Duncan Phyfe
But make no ridiculous mistakes in life,
And hear no laughter down the silly years.
Poor little wretches, and lucky little dears!

Elspeth

Sonnet

That same white traveller, frost, that could not pass
    And not leave everywhere his lovely scroll,
Having adorned sufficiently my glass,
    Painted your portrait on my secret soul.
Thus you've been with me all this winter day,
    And I, who love myself, went two and two,
My actual solitude a fancied play,
    Built of the meaning and the breath of you.

Of you each item in this day of fearing
    All thoughts I wanted to—and could not—tell;
You in the log of pine, you in my hearing
    That cold and holy ringing of a bell.
Your voice at sundown, swelling, repeating, thinning,
Lost in the hurrying night and the wind's beginning.

E. B. White

Love

G. Putnam's bookstore has designs
    On all our human hopes:
One window full of valentines,
    And one of Dr. Stopes.

E. B. White

For an Old Dance

What can be said
When we depart?
What can begin
When we are over?
For love, no mouth,
For grief, no tears.
O, learn me now,
Hearing me beat
Like sound in the ears,
Blood in the heart.
Quick, come away;
Be my lover.

Nothing can wait:
Not spring, the wind,
Not light, the flower.
All loves abate.
And quieter lying
Than grass struck down
On a winter hill,
I shall lie,
You will be still—
Than the fallen branch,
The leaf in the cold,
Locked in the snow
By dark closed over—

Come, be my lover;
We shall grow old.
Come away now.

Louise Bogan

Secret Joys

I

The poetry of mood and line
Was what excited Mr. Klein.
When trade was dull he used to hop,
Completely nude, around his shop,
Waving a blue linoleum rose
To balance each romantic pose.
Yet if a customer arrived,
This active Mr. Klein contrived
To dress so fast and look so grim
That no one ever spotted him.

II

The homely joys of fatherhood
Appealed so much to Mr. Wood
That though he felt averse to marriage
He bought himself a baby carriage,
And wheeled it with intense delight
Around his bedroom every night.

Clarence Day

Poem About Dogs

Till a dog breeder has taken a cup he's ardently busy in tending
his puppies.
Quits he perusing both Cabell and Gibbon—all for the sake of
a segment of ribbon.
Life cannot be, he says, gayer or merrier—raising a bloodhound,
a bull-dog or terrier.
Goes he to dog shows both haggard and worried—crates he in
dogs that are fine-combed and curried.

53

A judge in a morning coat studies and puzzles over the angles
of foreheads and muzzles.

Crowds peer in cages of eight, say, or say nine—fat ladies rave
over each single canine.

I'd never go of my private volition to any such silly and dull
exhibition.

Philip Wylie

More Preyed upon Than Preying

Bachelors should never be
Grudged their so-called liberty.
Margaret Fishback

III. MARCH: *With a scud of storm*

Sunday

The gentlemen's sticks swing extra high,
So sharp the air, so March the sky;
The gentlemen's steps are extra spry
And gentlemen's hats are silk and high,
  When Millicent takes me walking.

The lady-fairs' boots are zippered tight,
So bleak the wind, so near the night;
And lady-fairs' noses are red, not white:
It's hardly an advantageous light
  When Millicent takes me walking.

The little dogs' robes are buckled fast,
So chill the day, so swift the blast;
On three-skip-one they patter past,
Oh, little dogs' legs go extra fast
  When Millicent takes me walking!

The icicles cling to the funniest things,
To a red moustache, to a griffin's wings,
To the under side of a Buick's springs,
Oh, an icicle doesn't care where it clings
  When Millicent takes me walking!

Oh, gentlemen's sticks swing extra high,
And sharp the air and March the sky,
And lady-fairs' boots are zippered tight,
Oh, bleak the wind, oh, near the night!
And little dogs' robes are buckled fast,
So chill the day, so swift the blast,
And icicles don't care where they cling—
Yet Millicent says it will soon be Spring
When Millicent takes me walking!
              E. B. White

Song from New Rochelle

[WITH A REFRAIN TO BE CHANTED SOLEMNLY BY A CHORUS CONSISTING OF N. Y., N. H. & HARTFORD R. R. CONDUCTORS, PASSENGER AGENTS, AND JOHN COOLIDGE]

Monday's child is fair of face,
   And her chauffeur's a handsome fellow.
Tuesday's child is full of grace,
   So she gracefully hails a Yellow.
Wednesday's child has a red coupé,
   With a little black horn she toots,
But I was born on a Saturday,
   And Saturday's child commutes!

CHORUS:

No responsibility is assumed for errors in time tables
Nor for inconvenience or damage resulting from delayed trains
Or failure to make connections.

They that live on Washington Square
   May sleep as long as they please.
And they slumber deep and they slumber fair
   In the affluent Seventies.
In Tudor City, the good and mild
   Lie late with a brow serene,
But I am only Saturday's child
   So I get the eight-sixteen.

CHORUS:

Buy tickets before boarding trains, and avoid
Payment of extra charge.

The other girls go out to play
   In the fields of corn and clover.
And the other girls can always stay
   Until the party's over.

But just when the height is at its fun
  And the yodelers grow vocal,
I am the one who needs must run
  To catch the Stamford Local.
It's I that hostesses yearn to shelve;
  The Bridge-Table Blight am I.
(If Cinderella went home at twelve,
  She probably lived in Rye.)
Before the chorus has ceased to smile
  Or the maestro dropped his baton,
I am the lass in the middle aisle
  Who's trying to get her hat on.

O, gayety dwells
In the best hotels,
  But little to me it boots,
For I was born
On Saturday morn,
  And Saturday's child commutes.

CHORUS:
The schedules shown herein are subject
To change without notice.
                              Phyllis McGinley

On the Vanity of Earthly Greatness

The tusks that clashed in mighty brawls
Of mastodons, are billiard balls.

The sword of Charlemagne the Just
Is ferric oxide, known as rust.

The grizzly bear whose potent hug
Was feared by all, is now a rug.

Great Caesar's bust is on the shelf,
And I don't feel so well myself!
                              Arthur Guiterman

59

Afternoon

When I am old and comforted
　And done with this desire,
With Memory to share my bed,
　And Peace to share my fire.

I'll fold my hair in scalloped bands
　Beneath my laundered cap;
And watch my cool fragile hands
　Lie light upon my lap.

And I will wear a spriggèd gown
　With lace to kiss my throat.
I'll draw my curtains to the town,
　And hum a purring note.

And I'll forget the way of tears,
　And rock, and stir my tea.
But oh, I wish those blessèd years
　Were further than they be!
　　　　　　　Dorothy Parker

Homunculus

Oh, see what I have made!
A delicate, precious ruse
By which death is betrayed
And all time given use.

See this fine body, joined
More cleanly than a thorn.
What man, though lusty-loined,
What woman from woman born

Shaped a slight thing, so strong,
Or a wise thing, so young?
This throat shall yet have song
And words move on this tongue.

It lacks but life: some scent,
Some kernel of hot endeavor,
Some dust of dead content
Will make it breathe forever.

Louise Bogan

Then and Now

Even love-in-a-fog, love-in-a-cloud,
Is pain, but worse the pang of times remembered,
When the streets, the river, were bannered
With heaven, and the heart proud—
The heart that now like a trapped animal
Pants, rends, and cries aloud.
Were those years good? They were hardly to be borne.
Youth that was cloudy, foggy, clogged with grief.
Yet memory goes back, compassionate memory,
Who best knows how to forget, binds up the torn
And ragged places, washes every stain,
Cries: heart, you were happy, could you change this grief
For that old pain.
So love that is not love returns to repair
The loss of youth with strange regret for joy
That was not joy, and therewith grief grows bold.
The river, the streets, are changed,
The heavens above me are different, and the boy
Beside me will not know till he is old
How time, curing the heart, can bring it to despair.

Babette Deutsch

"My Child Is Phlegmatic . . ."—Anxious Parent

Anxious Parent, I guess you have just never been around;

I guess you just don't know who are the happiest people anywhere to be found;

I guess you just haven't ever been to the Beaux Arts or Kit Kat
or Cholly Knickerbocker or Old Guards Ball;

I guess you just haven't had any experience of life at all.

So you are worried, are you, because your child is turning out to
be phlegmatic?

Forgive me if I seem a trifle unsympathatic.

Why do you want your child to be a flashing, coruscating gem?

Don't you know the only peace the world can give lies not in
flame but in phlegm?

Don't you know that the people with souls of putty

Are the only people who are sitting prutty?

They never get all worked up at the drop of a pin or a feather
or a hat,

They never go around saying bitterly to themselves: "Oh God
did I really do, did I really say *that?*"

They never boil over when they read about stool pigeons getting
girls into reformatories by making treacherous advances;

They never get perfectly futilely harrowed about Sacco and Van-
zetti or Alice Adamses who don't have good times at dances;

They never blink an eyelash about colleges that are going to the
dogs because of football overemphasis;

They never almost die with indignation when some colored
person is lynched in Natchez or Memphis.

No, when they eat they digest their food, and when they go to
bed they get right to sleep

And four phlegmatic angels a solid watch over them keep.

Oh to be phlegmatic, oh to be stolid, oh to be torpid, oh to be
calm!

For it is only thus, Anxious Parent, that we can get through life
without a qualm.

Ogden Nash

To a Household Pet

You return
  From a weekend party
Looking wicked,
  Smug, and smarty.

From your manner
  I am very
Sure you've eaten
  A canary!

Yes, I see
  A yellow feather
On your coat.
  I wonder whether

When you're old
  You still will wander,
Rat around,
  And prowl out yonder?

Well, if you can't
  Live without it,
Nothing can be
  Done about it!
                    Angela Cypher

Monkey Business ×

Apes Taught Money Making.—*Headline.*

  Well,
  I'll have another try!
  If an ape can,
  Why can't I?
              Mildred Weston

63

Love's Enigma

Eros, your aural member bend!
  Hist! God of Passion, known as Cupid;
A knotty problem doth transcend
  The intellect of mortals stupid—
Why do the Better People hound
  With obloquy and stigma
The loves that make the world go round?
  Now *there* is an enigma!

The love of Typists for their Fat Employer,
Of Débutantes for their Papas' Chauffeurs,
Of Spinster for her Scoundrelly Annoyer,
Of Him Who's Getting Well for his Masseuse;
Of Orphan for his Wealthy Benefactress,
Of Chilled Explorer for the Eskimo,
Of Husband for the All-Uncovered Actress,
Of Dowager for Handsome Gigolo;
Of Model for the Artist with His Palette,
Of Swimmer for the Tar Who Saved Her Life,
Of Lonely Lady for her Husband's Valet,
Of Pompous Banker for the Cashier's Wife;
Of Nurse Who's On At Night for the Physician,
Of Freshman for his College Roommate's Aunt,
Of Nobody for Someone Of Position,
Of Catholic, Moslem, Jew for Protestant;
Of Sergeant's Daughter for the Reigning Hannibal,
Of Social Leader for the Indian Guide,
Of Stranded Missionary for his Cannibal,
Of Dressy Usher for the Bridegroom's Bride;
Of Curate for the Pretty Choir Singer,
Of Teacher for the Boy in Seventh Grade,
Of Schoolgirl for the Actor's Little Finger,
Of Virgin for the Hopeless Renegade;
And many more—I know a goodly store full—

They all are passions everyone laments;
We designate their character as awful,
And ostracize the fellow who dissents.

Now if it's true that mortal love
    Contributes to this planet's motion,
Why are we all so keen to shove
    Our hapless lovers in the ocean?
O, Cupid, God of Love, propound
    Why that must bear a stigma
Which makes the merry world go round?
    Now *there* is an enigma!

                                    Fillmore Hyde

And/Or

The Government gave Simeon Clay
Terrific headaches by the way
It made him fill out numerous blanks
Without a single word of thanks.
It even threatened, stern and grim,
To fine and/or imprison him
If he omitted to compile
The schedules which it loved to file.

Clay looked around, saw it was worse
And ever harder on the purse
In England, Finland, Yap, Siam,
The Argentine, and parts of Guam.
So off he went, a week ago,
To turn into an Eskimo,
Far in the North where cross officials
Will shriek in vain for his initials,
And where he will ignore their wishes
And live on ice and little fishes.

                                    Clarence Day

Just Off the Concrete

Now by the crossroads, in the filling station,
The boys assemble. Out of the winter night
Salting the stubbled face, peppering the lungs,
They enter the hot smell of burning wood,
And thawing wool, and heady gasoline.
The radio, the household imbecile,
Slavers and crows unheeded. Pop flows free.
And the old tales are told, born of the earth,
Ripened like grain, and harvested for winter.

It seems the village veterinarian
Suggested to the village constable
A little expedition after rabbits.
The constable, he likes a little shooting,
And so they met up at the doctor's house.
Well, Doc he had some prime old applejack,
And just in case they should get struck by lightning
Or something, why they hit it pretty hard.
Well, they were feeling good when they got started,
And when they got down by the Weaver place,
The Doc he says: "You see that cow in the pasture?
Bet you five dollars I could hit that cow,
Setting right here." "Well, bet you couldn't!"
The constable he says. And just like that,
The Doc he reaches back and grabs a rifle
Out of the back seat, and he draws a bead,
And drops that cow as dead as butcher meat!
"By gosh, I guess I *did* kill Weaver's cow!"
The Doc says. And "By gosh, I guess you did,
You gol-durn fool!" the cop says. Well, they turned
Around, and bust all records back to town,
And had a couple, quick. The constable
Went to the drugstore, and he bought some gum,
And hung around the rest of the afternoon,

66

Establishing, you know, an alibi.
It wasn't hardly evening when the sheriff
Went to the drugstore. All the boys were there.
And he goes right up to the constable,
And says to him: "Say, Alfred, where was you
At three o'clock this afternoon?" The cop
Says: "I was out to my garage, I guess.
My carburetor, she don't work so good."
"Then you ain't seen the vet?" the sheriff says.
"No, I ain't seen him, not since yesterday."
"You don't know who went hunting with the vet?"
"Gosh, no. I only know it wasn't me."
"Must have been someone looked a lot like you."
"Well, Judas priest, they's plenty looks like me."
"Well, I got witnesses to say 'twas you.
You ain't heard nothing, then, of Weaver's cow?"
"My gosh, I didn't know he had a cow!
I ain't been near the Weaver place today!
I swear I didn't touch his gol-durn cow!
If the vet says I did, I say he lies!
What happened to the durn cow, anyhow?"
"Why," says the sheriff, "Arthur Weaver says
He had to have her killed, she was so old,
And don't give down no more. And so the vet,
He went and shot her there this afternoon!"
Well, up to town the boys are laughing still.

Drowsiness gathers in the filling station.
Stirring their courage in the warmth and laughter,
The boys turn homeward. On the frozen ruts
Of the hill roads the little cars are shaken.
All the lights cease. The pond ice cracks with cold.

Morris Bishop

Portrait of a Gentleman

Ebenezer Winterfleece
Leaned against the mantelpiece
  And lit a cigarette.
  The samovar was set,
But no one poured the tea—
Yet through the candles he could see,
Between the candles flutteringly,
  Eager ladies frailly pass
  Nebulous as isinglass.
Ebenezer Winterfleece
Stroked the marble mantelpiece
  And with a rather nice alarm
  Recalled a certain person's arm.
Six candles glimmered in a row
Before a faint intaglio,
Beneath a wistful cameo
  That wasn't hanging straight.
  Someone passed a plate
Of golden macaroons—
Heaps of wrinkled moons
Matched with silver spoons.
  Every person he could see
  Blistered with gentility
  And hid behind a cup of tea.
Ebenezer Winterfleece
Posed before the mantelpiece;
Saw the architectured crease
  In his trousers and his coat.
  Tenderly he cleared his throat
And arched his brows at heaven.
Dinner was at seven—
  It seemed a year or two—
  The music tasted blue.
She played with such ethereal care,

As if her harp were made of air,
As if it really wasn't there—
  While in the room the gentlemen
  Were languorous for oxygen.
Ebenezer Winterfleece
Wondered if the mantelpiece
Came from Italy or Greece.
  But it was getting late,
  So stooping by the grate
He tossed his light away—
There was no need to stay.
  But from the door he still could see
  Between the candles flutteringly,
Eager ladies frailly pass
Nebulous as isinglass.

Herbert Gerhard Bruncken

To My Country

O curious acre, blossoming with gall,
Tender and terrible and sweet and crass;
Beloved bitterness, rock, custom, grass,
Untutored substance that knows nothing and all,
Ruin and freshness, serpent, scourge, and bird;
You with your stillborn look, you with your light
Surround me, you are day, you are heavy night,
You are a fresh mouth and a bitter word.

How could you matter, mattering not at all
To time's vague acreage? And numbering none
In the account that space keeps of the small,
How do you then outnumber anyone?
And yet you do, and I can hear you call
With the dear voice to my supposed free bone.

Raymond Holden

Paradox

I don't care how an author looks.
I only care about his books.
Whether he's living at Hyères,
Or sails a yacht, or braids his hair,
Or curls it, or keeps cawing rooks
About his castled towers, or cooks
His lunch himself in breakfast nooks,
                    I do not care.
If Kathleen Norris hangs on hooks
Or hangers or on shepherds' crooks
Her coats, if Dickens' son be fair
Or black, if on the stubble bare
The corn be stacked in shocks or shooks
About the fields of Van Wyck Brooks,
                    I do not care.
But many thousand things like these
Confront me, when I take my ease
And seek to learn of all the flow
Of many-minded books that go
About the earth and seven seas—
"What does the writer tell or know?"
Not "Are his taxes high or low?"
Nor "Does he motor fast or slow?"
Nor "Is his grandson swarming bees?"
Or many thousand things like these.
I don't care how an author looks.
I only care about his books.

And yet I read them high and low,
The gossip columns row on row—
Glance through them all, each blurb and wheeze
That tells me how the authors sneeze,
Or cough or cry or mop or mow,
And many thousand things like these.

                    Edith Franklin Wyatt

Portrait in Black Paint

WITH A VERY SPARING USE OF WHITEWASH

"She gives herself"; there's a poetic thought;
She gives you comfort sturdy as a reed,
She gives you fifty things you might have bought,
And half a hundred that you'll never need;
She gives you friendship, but it's such a bother,
You'd fancy influenza from another.

She'd give the shirt from off her back, except that
She doesn't wear a shirt and most men do;
And often and most bitterly she's wept that
A starving tramp can't eat a silver shoe,
Or some poor beggar, slightly alcoholic,
Enjoy with Donne a metaphysical frolic.

She gives away her darling secret hope
At dinner tables between eight and nine,
And she would give Saint Peter's to the Pope,
And coals to men of Newcastle-on-Tyne.
She would arrange a match for Solomon
Or give Casanova an adoptive son.

She does not give advice; that I admit;
Here's her sole virtue, and I'll count it double,
Forgiving her some crime because of it,
But she gives tiresome and endless trouble,
If you need rest, she'll straight contrive a racket;
If gaiety, she'll fetch a padded jacket.

And she gives love of the least useful kind
At which advanced civilization mocks;
Half, a platonic passion of the mind,
And half, a mad desire to mend the socks;

She's always wishing to turn back the page
And live with children in a golden age.

She gives a false impression that she's pretty
Because she has a soft deceptive skin
Saved from her childhood; yet it seems a pity
That she should be as vain of this as sin;
Her mind might bloom, she might reform the world
In those lost hours while her hair is curled.

She gives a vague impression that she's lazy,
But when she writes she grows intense and thorough;
Gone quietly and ecstatically crazy
Among the sea-blue hills of Peterboro',
She'll work within her cool, conventional flat
As self-sufficient as a Persian cat.

And she can live on aspirin and Scotch
Or British ginger beer and bread and butter,
And like them both, and neither very much;
And in her infancy she possessed a stutter
Which gives a strong impression that she's shy
When heard today, and this is verity.

But when she clothes herself in gold and silver
In the evening, she gives herself away;
Having remained a high laborious delver
For all the hours of a sunny day,
At night she gives you rather the idea
Of mad Ophelia tutored by Medea.

She gives you nothing worth consideration;
The effervescence of enthusiasm
Is trivial stuff; she'll give you adoration
If you belong to her peculiar schism;
As, that a certain English man of letters
Need never call the Trinity his betters.

Sometimes she gives her heart; sometimes instead
Her tongue's sharp side. Her will is quick to soften.
She has no strength of purpose in her head
And she gives up entirely too often;
Her manners mingle in disastrous ways
"The Lower Depths" and the Court of Louis Seize.

Doubtless, she gives her enemies the creeps
And all her friends a vast amount of worry;
She's given oblivion only when she sleeps;
She says she loves the grave; but she'd be sorry
To die, while it is a vanity to live;
"She gives herself"; what has she left to give?

She'd give her eyes—but both her eyes are blind—
And her right hand—but both her hands are weak—
To be "Careless to win, unskilled to find,
And quick—and quick—to lose what all men seek."
But whether this has truly been her story
She'll never know, this side of purgatory.

Elinor Wylie

Nothing Left

Something in me runs to meet
Everyone upon the street,
And I feel a subtle claim
If a friend but call my name.
Every object that I see
Carries off a part of me.
So with all this daily stress,
What is me grows less and less,
Till I wonder what will be
Left for immortality?
Harp and wings and crown to wear—
Nothing under them but air!

Alice Corbin

73

Reflections (in all Senses) on My Friends

When I see the awkward mating
Of my friends, I feel a grating

In my mind, a sort of blinking
At the most unpleasant linking

Of the charming and uncharming,
Of the witty and alarming

Types of mind that, bound together,
Go on biting at the tether.

How much better in our dining
Do we manage our combining!

With what sense the cook decrees
That the lamb must walk with peas;

That roast beef shall ever go
With the shapeless potato;

That the horrid, watery bean
Upon the heavy pork shall lean!

Unions these of art and plan,
Most unlike the work of man,

Where a mind of fresh green peas
Strives a roast-beef soul to please;

And mashed potatoes, fat and dread,
March gay lambkins home to bed;

While leering beans leap from the dish,
Forget the pork, and wink at fish.

Truly we must get a book
Entitled "Marriage," by the cook!

Hortense Flexner

Spook

Get out of my soup,
Get out of my tea,
I asked you to please
Keep away from me.

I want to forget
All about us two
But all over town
I encounter you.

It was here we dined,
It was there we sat
In a public lobby
For a private chat.

It was here we walked
In the leafy dark.
Go away. This isn't
Your personal park.

Stop haunting the streets.
It's a shame. It's a pity
To go on spoiling
The whole damn city.

Margaret Fishback

O. K., Parnassus

Writing is an interesting business, whether one pursues it as a vocation or merely as a sideline.—*Bruce Barton in a Farewell Address in the* Herald Tribune.

Oh, send up sky rockets by the carton!
   The Muse is endorsed by Mr. Barton!
The Pride of the *Tribune,* before his flitting
   Has set his seal on the writing game.
(Fascinating as flagpole-sitting,
   Though the technical background's not the same.)
Do seasonal fads begin to bore you?
Then writing's the positive hobby for you,
Keeping you out of the dews and damps,
Better than gathering postage stamps.
Are jig-saw puzzles as ashes and dust?
Does bridge fatigue? Then you simply must
Take up the recentest Sport of Kings.
Why, *everybody* is writing things.

Ring out, wild bells, the glorious tiding!
Poet and scribbler, burst from hiding!
Strum on your harp, and tune your tuba:
Writing's been recognized, just like Cuba.
Bruce approved it before he went
And syndicated his sentiment.
Mr. Barton, who sponsored God,
Has given Shakespeare a friendly nod;
Bowed to Milton, Montaigne, Defoe,
Slapped the back of Boccaccio,
And found a moment, though time was scanty,
To say an affable word for Dante.
"Writing," he cries with a stern elation,
"Is really an interesting occupation."

Phyllis McGinley

Wild Geese

Now, before the gaunt-limbed apple trees have bloomed,
Before maples flaunt their drooping crimson feathers,
On a day overcast, on a noon with a scud of storm,
While the air is half-gay, half-sad, and the grasses tug at their
    tethers,
Creeping with green around the roots of the orchard,
On a day remembering winter and waiting for spring,
Out of the south, out of that certain summer,
They come—the narrow of throat, the steady of wing!

The wild geese, trailing their legs on a leaden sky,
Their sharp, wild wings in a beautiful, lanky wedge,
Beat up from Virginia, up from the Chesapeake, driving
Like an arrowhead over Connecticut, over the edge
Of the troubled and northern spring!

You and I have much to remember—gulls
And cities and seas and the impending sense of loss;
And we shall have more as the years fly—parting and pain
And loneliness like a perpetual lash across
Our naked hearts; but always when we behold
The wild geese going northward, we shall touch
Briefly spirit to spirit, hearing their crying—
We shall meet swiftly . . . it will not be too much.

Frances Frost

Prelude

And that grin, the grin of the unfaithful,
the secret grin of self-congratulation
facing the mirror at midnight, when all has gone well,
when the returning footstep has not been heard,
nor the errand guessed, nor the change of heart perceived,
nor the eye's secret discovered, nor the rank perfume
smelled on hand or mouth

                              That grin like a flower
which opens voluptuously amid poisons and darkness
at the mere sight of itself as if to say
courage you have done it let now bravado
match in its brazenness the mercurial deception
go forth and kiss the cheek of her you have deceived

You too have known this and failed to be ashamed
have brazened it out and grinned at your own grin
holding the candle nearer that you might see
the essential horror.

                              Yes, and you have noted
how then the chemistry of the soul at midnight
secretes peculiar virtue from such poisons:
you have been pleased: rubbed metaphoric hands:
saying to yourself that the suffering, the shame,
the pity, the self-pity, and the horror
that all these things refine love's angel,
filth in flame made perfect.

                                        Conrad Aiken

To a Perfumed Lady at the Concert

Madam, the pervasive scent
    Rendering your person smelly
Formed a thick integument
    Round the music of Corelli.
        Lost on me the Sarabande.

Lady odorous and rare,
    You were such a proper noseful
All the brasses of "La Mer"
    Seemed by contrast quite reposeful.
        Lost on me the muted trumpet.

Baby drenched in fragrance vile,
  Scent in public may be legal
But it blanketed the guile
  Of a piece like "Eulenspiegel."
    Lost on me was Dicky Strauss.

Madam reeking of the rose,
  Red of hair and pearl of earring,
I came not to try my nose,
  I was there to try my hearing.
    Lost on me the whole darn concert.

Madam! Lady! Baby doll!
  This is what the world objects to:
Must you smell up all the hall
  Just to charm the guy you're next to?
    You were lost on him already.
                              E. B. White

The Sculpture Game

Some love Maillol. Some like most
Tidbits from the Ivory Coast.

Patriots in the Southern states
Like concrete Confederates.

Greek instructors flex their knees
To Scopas and Praxiteles.

Cryptic statements by Brancusi
Some find excellent, and juicy.

Busts of tin and brass and steel
Have a certain school to heel.

One likes sternly tetrahedral
Stuff; another, Chartres Cathedral.

And all, with clamorous huff and puff,
Combine to make things very tough

For young and simple souls who cope,
At best, with kittens cut from soap.

Price Day

IV. APRIL: *It is Spring! It is Spring!*
On the lea, on the ling!

The Satyr's Saturday Night

Gramercy Square is the properest square
  That ever ironed in
Its sacred turf, and it was there
  That I sinned an ill-bred sin.

'Twas the time of year when buds are new
  And spring comes on apace
That I issued out of the burlicue
  That is down in Irving Place.

A tender breeze was whispering;
  The evening shadows fell;
My brain was hot with youth and spring
  And life and Babe Lavelle.

And when I came to Gramercy Park
  With its iron fence around
I paused as one adream to hark
  To an unforgotten sound.

The vessels pounded in my head,
  A wild laugh filled my throat;
I heard the pipe of the capriped
  That plays upon an oat!

My breath became a vernal gale,
  A lightning charged my lymph,
For sitting there inside the pale
  I saw a taunting nymph!

(I had often passed by Gramercy Square
  And sometimes I had seen
Some well-bred dogs and children there
  Upon that guarded green,

And sometimes through the awesome gates
   I'd seen a maiden sad
With specs like William Butler Yeats',
   But never an oread.)

I leaped the iron barrier!
   I seized her by the waist!
Her startled lips were merrier
   Than brandy to the taste!

She broke away. She turned. She ran.
   Throughout my mad pursuit
I heard the oaten reed of Pan
   Go toot and tweedle-toot.

'Twas fleeing nymph and avid faun—
   Retreat and laughing lust,
While all the grave hotels looked on
   With dignified disgust.

I seized the ribbon that she wore
   About her neck—but nay!
She gave a jerk. The ribbon tore.
   My dryad got away.

I know not how I left the park
   Nor how I came to stand
Outside the gates in the growing dark
   With a ribbon in my hand,

But horror waited to perplex
   Me there outside the gates.
From the ribbon hung a pair of specs
   Like William Butler Yeats'.

Jake Falstaff

Pianola d'Amore

Sing hey, sing ho, and heigh-o,
From Calais, Maine, to Cal.,
For the blue that's in the sky-o,
For the will that's in the shall;

For the ding as in the dong-o,
For the larynx in the lad,
And the ping preceding pong-o,
And the sweet succeeding sad.

Sing April so embry-o
From Cal. to Calais, Maine,
And the little bow tie awry-o,
And the Queen of the Can't Complain.

Sing apple seed and cherry,
Sing cup and violet, too;
Sing riding on the ferry,
Sing visiting the zoo;

Sing popular, sing classic,
"Now doth the merry what?"
Sing tenor, boy, or bassic,
Or maybe better not.

Remain in Cal. or Calais,
And sing in either, Pal,
But down from Dak. to Dallas,
Pledge me a gill or gal.

And if in Cannes or Como
I hear you singing, say!
I'll sniff the sweet arom-o
And breathe another day.

David McCord

No Shampoo Today, Louis

Myself, I feel a dark despair
When I consider human hair
(Fine filaments sprouting from the skin),
I tremble like an aspirin.
For men and women everywhere
Unconsciously are growing hair,
Or, if the other hand you choose,
With every breath a hair they lose.
Unbid it cometh, likewise goeth,
And oftentimes it's doing boeth.
This habit is the chief determinant
Why permanent waves are less than permanent.
You rise, Madame, you face your mirror,
You utter cries of shame and terror.
What though to males you look all right?
For heaven's sake, your hair's a sight.
You hasten to the Gallic lair
Where lurks Maurice or Jean or Pierre.
Between arrival and departure,
You suffer hours of vicious torture,
At last emerging white and weak,
But sure at least your mane is chic.
Thus you rejoice, my dear, unknowing
That all the time your hair is growing.
The wave so dearly purchasèd
Next month will have grown a foot or so
                              away from your head.

I face mankind and shudder, knowing
That everybody's hair is growing;
That lovers, linked in darkened hallways,
Are capped with hair that groweth always;
That millions, shaven in the morning,
At eve find beards their jowls adorning;

That hair is creeping through the scalps
Of yodelers yodeling in the Alps,
And pushing through the epidermises
Of peasants frolicking at kermises,
And poking bravely through the pores
Of cannibals on tropic shores;
That—freezing, scorching, raining, snowing—
People's hair is always growing.
I contemplate with dark despair
The awful force of growing hair,
Although admitting, to be quite honest,
That it will be worth a million Niagaras to humanity
      if Science can ever get it harnessed.

Ogden Nash

Many a Night

Many a night, many a night,
  A million years ago,
Stars, as now, were cold and bright
  When I was feeling low.
A faithful hound beside me,
  My lovely bride asleep,
I'd sigh for boons denied me
  And stare at space and weep.

I don't recall what made me stare
  Or why I felt so glum.
We all have moods of vague despair,
  And moods like that are rum.
Tonight again I can't decide
  What's causing me regrets.
Is it perhaps my present bride?
  My liver? Or my debts?

Clarence Day

Ballad of Little Faith

At certain times in every day
I seem about to write a play
  So deeply true,
  So fine, so new,
 So full of all humanity
That it will write itself in fire
And send my stocks a whole lot higher
  And brand me mad,
  A wondrous lad,
 And vindicate my vanity.

Sing ho, sing hey, sing ho, sing hey,
The young man thinks he'll write a play,
But only at certain times of day!

When I sit down with proper zeal
To write the play I really feel,
  Gird on the pen
  With strength of ten
 And try to do some thinking,
I find it's time to pay a call,
Or put the laundry in the hall,
  Or kiss a maid,
  Or build my trade,
 Or do a little drinking.

Sing ho, sing hey, sing ho, sing hey,
He thinks he'd like to write a play,
But only at certain times of day.

Perhaps if I could write one line
That all the world could see was fine,
  One perfect phrase

To ease my days
And make my nights effectual,
I'd give up love and food and friends
And dreams and life and means-to-ends,
And brood and brood
In solitude
Entirely intellectual.

Sing ho, sing hey, sing ho, sing hey,
He wants to brood and write a play,
But only at certain times of day.

With plays by men who catch their stride
By dint of turning life aside,
Foregoing all,
A kiss, a call,
I never have been smitten;
But while I hold them deep in scorn
And still stay out each night till morn,
It's not amiss
That I say this:
Those plays at least get written!

Sing ho, sing hey, sing ho, sing hey,
He knows he'll never write a play—
Except at certain times of day!

E. B. White

Thought for a Sunshiny Morning

It costs me never a stab nor squirm
To tread by chance upon a worm.
"Aha, my little dear," I say,
"Your clan will pay me back one day."

Dorothy Parker

Brownstone:
An Elegy

Vanishing screen, as dismal and opaque
   As ever public gaze was shattered on,
Petrified soul of dullness, for whose sake
   Were ravished the fair hills of Portland (Conn.),

Farewell to you! Stupid and sumptuous
   You reigned, nor brick nor granite dared rebel;
But you encased the world that dawned on us,
   And so to you, and to that world, farewell!

Farewell the curlicues, the filigrees!
   Farewell the lockets, lambrequins and loops,
And scraps of tissue paper that the breeze
   Blew from gloved hands down your proud-arching stoops!

Farewell the boas, the bustles and the broughams,
   The tight frock-coats and clove-sweet breath of men
Who "popped the question" in dim drawing-rooms
   That your dank bosom mothered like a hen!

Farewell the nine-course dinners, the Sauterne,
   The ever-pinching, never-mentioned stays;
The songs, the slang, the sleigh-rides that we spurn
   But cheered the reign of Rutherford B. Hayes!

Farewell, stern chocolate vistas! Never more
   Shall you confuse the tired provincial eye.
In chintz and limestone, on the fortieth floor,
   Our shrill domestic pageant clatters by,

With half a tear for you, and half a pain,
   Such as evokes a father's friend's decease—
And long may all your virgin kin remain
   In Portland (Conn.)'s remote Triassic peace!
                    Wayland Wells Williams

Sonnets to Baedeker

I

My old companion on the beaten track,
Who brought me villages and bed and board,
Settled the day and laid me on my back
At inns whose tariff I could not afford;
Sweet *vade mecum* of the *Tuileries,
And audible in naves and barrel vaults,
Still smelling of an earlier Cheddar cheese,
Or blemished with red wines and English malts;
So I remember with what crafty charm
Of small italics and appropriate miles
Distinguished pages loosened a new swarm
Of ancient *Ninevehs* and distant *Niles*,
And played upon my mind as men at chess,
And sold me to AMERICAN EXPRESS.

II

Once it was Paris of *la Reine Pédauque*,
With *SACRÉ-CŒUR like loaves of a young yeast,
And people trading in a foreign talk
For seriatims of the *bouquiniste*.
O glory then upon the face of France:
Who painted what, and where the most is hung,
Such royal chambers of strange occupance
As burned to envy the guide's eager tongue.
Figures and dates assigned at *ST-SULPICE,
And when the garlic boats ran down the *Seine;*
Recumbent *Abélard and Héloïse,*
The streets that saw a thousand Shelleys plain.
Fine view (adm. gratis). Was it Psyche?
Or Cook's own clients round the nerveless **Nike?

91

III

Patron of *char-à-bancs* and steamer chair,
Whose roads and rivers coruscate the land;
And who, with the shy word of de la Mare,
Impute delight on every other hand;
Give me a voyage, payable in marks,
As favoring T̲ɪ̲ᴛ̲ɪ̲s̲ᴇ̲ᴇ̲ and Rhenish town,
With Goethe, Schiller, sodium baths, and parks,
Or citadel of century-ripened brown;
Musik im Garten, Ha! zu **Düsseldf.**—
Soothingest wherefore to each alien why!
History recollecting at the wharf
Old fatal interviews with ***Lorelei;**
And Germans clambering over Iliad forts,
So well binoculared and wearing shorts.

They called him Ishmael. I call you Karl,
Who printed London on a Leipzig press,
And left delirious in simple snarl
What most obliges of her great noblesse.
Out of red covers wells the million sound
Of man and lorry over Oxford Circ.,
And from the purlieus of the underground
The actual Londoners emerge to work.
Sweet catalogue, beyond the last inhab.
Who dwell in **Claridges* and Bᴇʀᴋᴇʟᴇʏ Sǫs.,
Or blithe Americans by taxicab
Ascending thus her golden British stairs—
Open to **Simpson's* and a London play,
And let me read and eat my heart away.

Then up to **Bicester** and the English towns:
Hail *Royal George (Pl. a; B, 4) and how!
Green separate spots of separate renowns,
As where some stout Archbp. made his vow.
Perp. churches, sir, cathedrals, E. E. style,
Castles to open Wed. 10-3;
Or Roman ruins of a domicile,
And *Keeps,* 12th cent. (restored), for a small fee.
Number of miles to Tottenham and back
(*Cycle or motorbus, afoot or train*),
The kind of villages one used to sack,
And what the Duke said to the King of Spain;
Who died wherever, and God rest their bones,
And why the *Druids* left such funny stones.

VI

But chief, in the moist latitudes of Skye,
You burred the difficult names of Scottish breed:
Blairgowrie, Tomnahurich, Morven—aye,
Of glens and invers to the trouty *Tweed.*
The grandest moors upon the purpled airth,
A Celtic twilight, and Midlothian heart
Commingle sadly in the sound of 'Perth'
As strong rfmt. offered by a bart.
Good patient soul, you spelled the Gaelic word,
Say *usquebaugh* for whiskey, in the notes;
Selected curlew, gannets, the wild bird
That screams the cowried shore by John o' Groats;
And where *Auld Reekie* stands eternal guard
You led me to the city ***triple-starred.

David McCord

Song to the Empire State Building

Goggle-eyed,
    The centuries con
The yet-enduring
    Parthenon.

To Chichen-Itzá
    And to Ur
Still the dumb
    Idolater

Goes, to stare
    At ziggurat
And tower whose beauty
    Dieth not.

But you, my darling,
    Stand and flame
A little while.
    Then your name,

Your pride, your glory,
    Crumble down,
Forgotten,
    In the furious town.

Pale cereus
    Abloom at night,
Or the frail gnat
    That knows one flight

And dies—as these
    Are lovelier
For haste, so you,
    Belovèd, are.

Wherefore my heart
So blithely sings
The excellence
Of fragile things.
                                Price Day

Letter to Mr. Pulitzer

Dear Mr. Pulitzer: I beg to mention
A thing that now demands your best attention
Since Fate has left you free and office-catless
And probably as much relieved as Atlas
When Hercules removed from his broad shoulders
The World with all its hills and nubbly boulders.
A lady is involved, so it's essential
To keep this matter strictly confidential.

Because your father gave it her, she has a
Delightful place before the Hotel Plaza;
"Die schönste Jungfrau" (please excuse the German),
Upon a fountain facing General Sherman,
The mists of morning draped around her, clammily,
This lady stands—a member of your family
By name, at least; I trust I do not bull it, sir,
But we have always called her "Mrs. Pulitzer."

One hates to speak this way about a lady,
But she is obviously much too shady;
Though still quite young, a good bit under thirty,
No nymph was ever quite so black and dirty
In all New York; so you, sir, as her guardian
(You see I'm Mid-Victorian, not Edwardian),
Should personally scrub her form and face in
The sudsy foam of her own fountain basin.
                                Arthur Guiterman

95

Parable for a Certain Virgin

Oh, ponder, friend, the porcupine;
    Refresh your recollection,
And sit a moment, to define
    His modes of self-protection.
How truly fortified is he!
    Where is a beast his double
In forethought of emergency
    And readiness for trouble?
Recall his figure and his shade;
    How deftly planned and clearly
For slithering through the dappled glade
    Unseen, or pretty nearly!
But should an alien eye discern
    His presence in the woodlands,
How little has he left to learn
    Of self-defense! My good lands!
For he can run as swift as sound
    To where his goose may hang high;
Or thrust his head against the ground
    And tunnel half to Shanghai;
Or he can climb the dizziest bough—
    Unhesitant, mechanic—
And resting, dash from off his brow
    The bitter beads of panic;
Or should pursuers press him hot
    One scarcely needs to mention
His quick and cruel barbs, that got
    Shakespearean attention;
Or, driven to his final ditch,
    To his extremest thicket,
He'll fight with claws and molars (which
    Is not considered cricket).
How amply armored he, to fend
    The fear of chase that haunts him!

How well prepared our little friend!
—And who the devil wants him?

Dorothy Parker

Cobbler

He mends the shoes
and watches the feet
of the crowd that goes
along the street.

A basement deep
and a sidewalk high;
along the ceiling
the feet go by;

toeing and heeling
they seem to skim
the top of the larky
world to him

in the dusty dark,
whose eyes dilate
as he gazes up
through the dingy grate.

The world hobbles
on feet of clay,
the cobbler cobbles
his days away;

crooked heels
and broken toes
are all he feels,
all he knows.

Peggy Bacon

I'm Proud to Admit That I'm Blushing:
A Sob Ballad

I

A crowd of "Ritzy" youngsters
   Who had danced the night away,
In Childs had stopped for breakfast.
   Their spirits still were gay.
As they ate their talk was "sexy,"
   There were risqué tales and verse,
Which were greeted with loud laughter
   As they went from bad to worse.
But one girl seemed uneasy,
   And when her cheeks with shame grew red,
A youth was quick to note it,
   And tauntingly he said:
"Well, see Baby Belle, *she's* blushing.
   I swear she's going to cry.
Did we shock you?" Here she stopped him
   And thus bravely did reply:

REFRAIN

"I'm proud to admit that I'm blushing—
   You may say, if you like, I'm a prude—
At your stories, your jokes, and your verses,
   Which I think just disgusting and lewd.
With so much in life that's engaging,
   It would seem to me—once in a while—
Some relief you might find in a subject refined,
   Unless you *prefer* to talk vile."

Her reply—so unexpected—
  Brought silence to them all,
Though *some* showed slight resentment
  And said, "Her bluff let's call."
But spoke one, a lad more thoughtful,
  "Belle is right, we ne'er discuss
A thing that's *halfway* decent;
  And I doubt if *one* of us
Has brains enough to do it,
  But by Gad! I'm going to try.
Come, Belle, let's go. One convert
  You've made and that is I."
And so firm was his conversion
  That before a month had fled,
His bride to be she'd promised,
  For he loved her when she said:

REFRAIN

"I'm proud to admit that I'm blushing—
  You may say, if you like, I'm a prude—
At your stories, your jokes, and your verses,
  Which I think just disgusting and lewd.
With so much in life that's engaging,
  It would seem to me—once in a while—
Some relief you might find in a subject refined,
  Unless you *prefer* to talk vile."

Clarence Knapp

Couplet

Girls who go to dinner "Dutch"
Never will amount to much.

Dorothy Dow

The Willingness

The willingness that Lucy wears
Becomes her like a fitted gown;
Nor is there any seam to see
Until the thing is down—
The whole of it, as if a lone
Young tree had cast its crown.

Those leaves that make so loose a ring
Will never again be hung together.
The flying bird does not regain
A single drifted feather.
So Lucy stands forever now
Unlaced against the weather.

The willingness that Lucy wore
Was nothing to this naked side.
And yet the truth of her is both;
The raiment never lied.
Desire without, desire within—
So is love simplified.

Mark Van Doren

Carillon

"Down with wild orgies!"
Says the bell of St. George's.

"Likewise French balls,"
Says the bell of St. Paul's.

"Censor theatrics!"
Says the bell of St. Patrick's.

"Spare harmless larks!"
Says the bell of St. Mark's.

"Make them no promises,"
Says the bell of St. Thomas's.

"Let's print our plans,"
Says the bell of St. Ann's.

"Think how they'll column you!"
Say the bells of Bartholomew.

"Fear no rebukes!"
Says the bell of St. Luke's.

"Sheer asininity!"
Says the bell of Old Trinity.

"File your complaints,"
Says the bell of All Saints'.

Arthur Guiterman

The Shower Bath

This rite none living shall disdain.
  Within this shrine all heads are bowed,
Primeval worshippers of rain,
  The hot, the weary, and the proud
Freshen for mischief or for rest,
  Feeling deliverance sublime
Beat on the burden of the breast.
  This is the thought as old as Time—
Thus, in the primal solitude
  That darkened Eden ere its fall,
Ventured the unassuming nude,
  To stand beneath a waterfall.

Persis Greely Anderson

The Law of the Jungle

Mr. Hemingway said that he shot only lions that were utter strangers to him.—*The Herald Tribune*.

When hot for sport and ripe to kill,
The average novelist shoots at will;
But that, my friends, I'm glad to say,
Is not the case with Hemingway,
Whose sporting life is ever so subtle
Where leopards roam and lions scuttle,
Whose fowling piece doth never bungle
The oldest law of Afric's jungle,
Who stands his ground in time of danger
But only shoots a total stranger.

What sort of cad, I ask, is he
Who meets a cat one day at tea
And next day, in the play of ire,
Cannot control his rifle fire?
Whose morals are so frightfully weird
He dens a lion in his beard
And shoots, to show that he knows how to,
A jungle beast he used to bow to,
Or massacres, in thoughtless wrath,
The first old pal to cross his path?

Ah, friends, beware the sportsman fickle
Whose four-foot friends aren't worth a nickel,
Whose ethics of the chase are phony,
Whose dachshunds are so much boloney;
And cling to Ernest Hemingway,
Who writes by night and hunts by day,
Whose books with gore are fairly ruddy
But *not* with gore of pal or buddy,
And who, in time of darkest danger,
Will only dominate a stranger.

E. B. White

The Passionate Pagan and the Dispassionate Public:
A Tragedy of the Machine Age

Boys and girls,
Come out to play,
The moon is shining
Bright as day.

If the moon is shining
Bright as day,
We think that we'll
Stay in and play.

Hey nonny nonny!
Come, Jennie! Come, Johnnie!
The year's adolescent!
The air's effervescent!
It bubbles like Schweppes!
Aren't you going to take steppes?

It's one of the commoner
Vernal phenomena.
You may go wild
Over air that is mild,
But Johnnie and Jennie
Are not having any.

It is Spring! It is Spring!
Let us leap! Let us sing!
Let us claim we have hives
And abandon our wives!
Let us hire violins
To belittle our sins!
Let us loll in a grotto!
Let this be our motto:

Not sackcloth, but satin!
Not Nordic, but Latin!

Hark to the radio!
Listen to KDO!
Tell us that Luna
Compares with that cruna.
Away with your capers!
Go peddle your papers!

It is Spring! It is Spring!
On the lea, on the ling!
The frost is dispersed!
Like the buds let us burst!
Let the sap in our veins
Rush like limited trains!
Let our primitive urges
Disgruntle our clergies,
While Bacchus and Pan
Cavort in the van!

Spring is what winter
Always gazinta.
Science finds reasons
For mutable seasons.
Can't you react
With a little more tact?
Please go and focus
Your whims on a crocus.

It is Spring! Is it Spring?
Let us sing! Shall we sing?
On the lea, on the ling
Shall we sing it is Spring?
Will nobody fling
A garland to Spring?

Oh, hey nonny nonny!
Oh, Jennie! Oh, Johnnie!
Doesn't dove rhyme with love
While the moon shines above?
Isn't May for the wooer
And June for l'amour?
No, it couldn't be Spring!
Do not dance! Do not sing!
These birds and these flowers,
These breezes and bowers,
These gay tirra-lirras
Are all done with mirrors!
Hey nonny! Hey nonny!
Hey nonny! Hey nonny!
Hey nonny! Hey nonny!
Hey nonny . . .

Ogden Nash

Litany

No, halt the step of Spring on earth, dear God.
Spare me the gentleness of April rain,
The tender spread of green upon the sod,
The eloquence of leaf—not that again!
Deliver me from winds too flower-sweet,
From love, emboldened by the touch of Spring,
From beauty, stepping down my humble street,
From youth, from innocence—from everything
Which would dissolve my spirit's thrall of frost.
Once loosed from Winter's fastness, man and earth
Must face again old dreams far better lost,
And feel once more the travail-pains of birth.
Good Lord, deliver me from love and truth;
Spare me, good Lord, the dreams of eager youth.

Elspeth

This Side of Summer

The little fists of grass fingering bright air,
The sturdy stems of young trees, silver and black,
Seem so sufficient that they need not care
How often foot or frost may push them back.
Yet the world, patched and tinkered with, were lame
Without the alien mind's embellishment.
It would not turn, it would not have a name,
Did merely loveliness provide content.
The heart is strong enough to bear the mind,
To go like horse and rider, the mind mounted.
The heart is strong because the sun is kind
And does not count the days that we have counted.
Because of something which can understand
That half of life the other cannot see
I touch the grass, the soft bark, take your hand
And live like air, who am not half so free.
Forget a while the pinch of being human,
The economy of age, the wheel, the lever,
The stones heaped round the lives of man and woman,
The tones of breath that frame the sound of never.
This is the morning of the middle day
That wears a clear and meadow-brightening light.
The grass, the tree, have put the winter away.
We, too, stand safe between two halves of night.

Raymond Holden

Twelve Good Men and True

Juror Five appears a little
Set in favor of acquittal.
Number One, in contradiction,
Leans to swift and sure conviction.
Three (a shipping clerk) is rather

Bored with all the fuss and bother.
Number Ten, a dapper fellow,
Notes the plaintiff's shoes are yellow.
Six (Augustus Miller, tanner)
Doesn't like the judge's manner.
Seven, weary-eyed, unfeeling,
Counts the fissures in the ceiling.
Twelve, who's quite unused to collars,
Wonders how he'll spend four dollars.
Number Eight, old hand at trying,
Thinks the witnesses are lying,
And Eleven, dozing, nodding,
Is a mark for constant prodding.
Number Two (bricklayer, married)
Thinks the County's point is carried.
Nine, who's bound for Queens for dinner,
Hopes his horse came in a winner.
Juror Four (three sons, one daughter)
Only wants a glass of water.

Parke Cummings

O Pity Poets

O pity poets everywhere—
With earth Intolerably Fair,
With love always Too Big to Bear.
These tender ones are far from proud:
A normal ordinary cloud
Will often make them cry out loud.
Sunsets, it seems, are extra sad.
A moon can drive them nearly mad.
In love they take on very bad.
A scrubby dandelion will bring
The briny tears. The bards can wring
White hands about most anything.

O does it not seem hard to you
What the pale poets must go through?
Now me on love I am not sold,
And Mother Nature leaves me cold.
There's not a scene that I could sigh for.
There's not a gent that I could cry for.
I may be rough, I may be wild,
I'm just a poor dog catcher's child,
But every single day I live
I thank God I'm not sensitive.

Jacqueline Embry

The Constant Jay

Oh, will a day, I wonder, ever be
When S. Jay Kaufman does not write to me!
Some days he just solicits information
Regarding where I'm going next vacation.
Some days he asks me (absolutely solemn)
To lay my work aside and write his column.
Some days he wants ten dollars, bucks or beans,
To help the starving Middle-Europeans.
I count that day a flop on land or sea
When S. Jay Kaufman does not write to me!

Ring Lardner

Manhattan Epitaphs:
Lawyer

He sent so many
to jail for life,
so many
to sudden death,
he finally lost
his own private case
because he was out of
breath.

Alfred Kreymborg

108

v. MAY: *Birds toot sweet on every bough*

Arctic Agrarian

[SCENE: THE ADIRONDACKS]

Here in these hills the Spring comes slow
  To those who learn her backward way,
Who plough in ice and reap in snow.

First, there's a tremor; then, a throe;
  Then splintering of bells that play
"Hear!" (In these hills the Spring comes slow.)

We are not tricked for long. We know
  The paradox of frost in May,
Who plough in ice and reap in snow.

A mole sniffs the new earth; a crow
  Measures our field, decides to stay.
Here in these hills the Spring comes slow.

These are our vernal auguries. We go,
  Stopping at times to curse or pray,
Who plough in ice and reap in snow.

Suddenly white is green, although
  When it occurred we cannot say,
Who plough in ice and reap in snow,
Here in these hills . . .
                    The Spring comes slow.
                        Louis Untermeyer

Natura in Urbe

While midnight clung to every shore
I walked me round the reservoir,
With little cause and little sense
I ambled round and round the fence,
And once, while standing quietly,
I saw a little duck swim by.

I plainly saw his head a-wobble,
I plainly saw his tail a-bobble,
As all across the captive lake
He spread his negligible wake.
And I can scarce begin to tell
How mystical this caravel,
Or how surprised I was to see
A duck as wide awake as me.

Afloat at night upon the deep
You'd think a duck would go to sleep,
You'd think a normal duck would hanker
To close his eyes and ride at anchor;
You'd think a duck would set his breast
Against the wave, and come to rest;
You'd think that twelve o'clock were late
For any duck to navigate
All round and round the reservoir.
I wondered what he did it for.

I wondered if he'd left his kind
Because of something on his mind,
A midnight sail to clear his vision
And help him reach some duck decision.
Surely he would not swim and swim
Were something hard not troubling him.
It was preposterous to think

A duck would rouse to get a drink;
Nor was it anything but silly
To think he paddled willy-nilly;
And though 'twas funny to suppose
A little duck had secret woes,
And though it put me on my mettle
To guess what problems ducks must settle,
I liked to think he swam the deep
Because he simply *could not* sleep.

E. B. White

For a Good Girl

[for D. P.]

Two tasks confront King Honour's daughter
Whom the unlearned malign insult;
One clear and luminous as water,
The other stiff and difficult.

Pity is laid upon the noble
So plain an obligation
Its fair performance is no trouble;
The puzzle's in the other one.

To be recognizant of merit
Peculiar to yourself; to be
Chivalric to your stronger spirit
Which gives the weak impunity.

This is the mental arabesque you
Must constantly contrive within,
Or how shall you survive to rescue
The little wicked from their sin?

Elinor Wylie

Rhyme of an Involuntary Violet

When I ponder lovely ladies
Slipping sweetly down to Hades,
Hung and draped with glittering booty—
Am I distant, cold and snooty?
Though I know the price their pearls are
Am I holier than the girls are?
Though they're lavish with their "Yes's,"
Do I point, and shake my tresses?
No! I'm filled with awe and wonder.
I review my every blunder. . . .
Do I have the skill to tease a
Guy for an Hispano-Suiza?
I can't even get me taxis
Off of Sydneys, Abes, and Maxies!
Do the pretty things I utter
To the kings of eggs and butter
Gain me pearls as big as boulders,
Clattering, clanking round my shoulders,
Advertising, thus, their full worth?
No, my dear. Mine come from Woolworth.
Does my smile across a table
Win a cloak of Russian sable?
Baby, no. I'd have to kill a
Man to get a near-chinchilla.
Men that come on for conventions
Show me brotherly attentions;
Though my glance be fond and melting,
Do they ever start unbelting
With the gifts they give the others?
No! They tell me of their mothers,
To the baby's pictures treat me,
Say they want the wife to meet me!
Gladly I'd be led to slaughter
Where the ermine flows like water,

Where the gay white globes are lighted;
But I've never been invited!
So my summary, in fact, is
What an awful flop my act is!

Dorothy Parker

Tombstones in the Starlight

I. THE MINOR POET

His little trills and chirpings were his best.
  No music like the nightingale's was born
Within his throat; but he, too, laid his breast
  Upon a thorn.

II. THE PRETTY LADY

She hated bleak and wintry things alone;
  All that was warm and quick, she loved too well—
A light, a flame, a heart against her own;
  It is forever bitter cold in Hell.

III. THE FISHERWOMAN

The man she had was kind and clean
  And well enough for every day,
But, oh, dear friends, you should have seen
  The one that got away!

IV. THE ACTRESS

Her name, cut clear upon this marble cross,
  Shines, as it shone when she was still on earth;
While tenderly the mild, agreeable moss
  Obscures the figures of her date of birth.

Dorothy Parker

A Recluse Contemplates Vagabondia

Dirty old gypsies
With handkerchiefs and bangles,
A few tin pots
And a caravan that jangles.
Who'd be a gypsy? Not I,
Although I love the open road
And sky.
Give me clean sheets
And a grate fire;
Better, say I,
Than rain and mire.
Give me a tub
In a porcelain room;
Give me a garden
With flowers in bloom.
Let me have a trellis
And roses growing;
Let me close the doors
When the wind is blowing.
I want no painted wagon
Creaking through the lanes,
Nor a leaky tent
When it rains.
Frowsy old gypsies,
Lousy and bitten,
No bed to lie upon,
No chair to sit in.
Mouching o'er the countryside,
Lagging in a ditch,
Steering for a farmer's light
When the night is pitch.
Take it all and keep it all,
Creep along the highway;
Wander o'er the world and back,
But I'll keep to my way.

Rollin Kirby

Mid-May Song

Now mid-May's here and I contrive
To add two twos and make them five,
Knowing, as I have known before,
The first of June will make them four.
Meanwhile, the loud, mammalian earth
Imbues with her priapic mirth
The hippopotamus and flea,
The queer baboon, the cruising bee,
The caterpillar on the tree,
The proud giraffe (who knows that he
Is modern architecturally)—
Imbues, in short, with springtime all
The Kingdom of the Animal,
Save one, whose maladjusted span
Constitutes the Life of Man.

While birds toot sweet on every bough,
And grass-grown yearnings fill the cow
With milk (grade A), and even cream,
And things are maybe what they seem,
And chickens, tipsy with the May,
Lay and lay and lay and lay
And lay (lay off; go on from here!)
And jolly mid-May flies appear,
In perfect harmony with all
On which they chance to light or fall,
And more successful upside down
Than any leading man in town—
While this occurs, and even more,
From shore to (naturally) shore,
And tick and tiger, bee and bear
Make vernal whoopee everywhere,
The lord of Science and the Arts,
Self-sung for various noble parts—

No less than Man himself I mean—
Continues to perplex the scene
And make the startled spring go boom
With antic *gesta hominum;*
With isms, schisms, cults, and creeds;
With febrile itches, phantom needs;
With saws and laws and cant and prayer;
With graft and craft and greed and care;
With freakish use and monster skill;
With idiot goal and maniac will;
With spires and swords and leagues and wars
And surfs of talk on sandy shores;
With *in hoc signo* on a Sunday
And *caveat emptor,* starting Monday;
With crumpled calf of stock and bond,
And keyhole prurience for Beyond
(While here the massive pain of Christ,
By Jews in Russia sacrificed,
Is parcel'd in the Baptist sticks
Into jolly bishoprics),
With sour achieving, harried striving,
Belly pacts and spleen conniving,
With—halt! survey the dimpled sight,
And catalogue your own delight.

Of all who labored from the slime
Under the dogged feet of Time,
And strove with ineluctable might
To straggle through the aqueous night,
Through vitreous frost and filmy green,
To some unnamable serene,
While past slipped into crackling past,
Is this, is Man, the first or last?
Has not the ape contrived to reach
Past lucky strike and Babel speech,
And all the quicksands of the mind

(His serio-comic world behind),
A pride, a place, a peace more stanch
In his plain Heaven of a branch?
Has not the tree itself attained
Its topmost powers, and stands ordained
In priesthood of harmonious place?
Before it found an equal grace,
What conquered worlds behind the bird
Of cactus Deed and tidal Word?
Is not, most ancient of the stock,
The rock melodious to the rock
Of human woes and human pains
Remembered in its empty veins?
Is there no wisdom wiser than
The fret, the fear, the whine of Man?

Well, mid-May's here and I contrive
To add two twos and keep alive,
And ponder Plato, now a fly,
Upon his ceiling of a sky.

Samuel Hoffenstein

Juan's Song

When beauty breaks and falls asunder
I feel no grief for it, but wonder.
When love, like a frail shell, lies broken,
I keep no chip of it for token.
I never had a man for friend
Who did not know that love must end.
I never had a girl for lover
Who could discern when love was over.
What the wise doubts, the fool believes—
Who is it, then, that love deceives?

Louise Bogan

Portrait

Here are the green pavilions of the spring.
Soft from the branches calls the deathless bird.
The young trees tremble; waters fall and sing;
The blunt root swells; the lily's leaves have stirred.

This is a forest so by love designed,
So filled with music and the sun's delight,
That all the longing of the amorous mind,
The heart's numb grief, the soul's aching flight

Are answered here where neither death nor pain
Troubles the wind with crying, where the blood
Sings at its running, where the falling rain
Is scented ever with the opening bud.

Here thought is one with loving; light with dark;
Dreaming with waking; moon and star are one;
Their harmonies the echo of the lark
That soars above this Eden to the sun.

Oh here, where life is laughter in the ground,
Here, where love's a blossom on the tree,
Time is but the setting and the sound
For one who moves to immortality.

Harold Lewis Cook

Advice to Parents

When bantlings brabble in their play
On any dull or brumous day,
To send them to a barracoon
Will quite upset their afternoon.

The cause of brabblement may be
A form of simple bulimy;

120

Some bigaroons or biffins will,
In normal cases, cure this ill.

But, if the state persists, do not
Threaten with bogles on the spot;
Psychiatrists, as one, decree
Against bashibazoukery.

But rather take them in a bandy,
Provided that you have one handy,
To watch the brahma-pootras', brents',
And butterbumps' accomplishments,

Or else procure a billyboy
And let the little dears enjoy
The barbel, brill, and bummalo
That frolic when the tide is low.

And if, by chance, you feel at night
A bittock like a bedlamite,
Some bhang or bumbo in a cup
Will do a lot to set you up.

Noah Webster and
Miriam Vedder

Four A. M.

My heart was broken
At half-past ten;
By midnight
I was drunk again.
At four o'clock
When I got home
I liked it better:
Being alone.

The room was dusty;
On the floor,
Newspapers left
A week or more,
Electric bulbs
That wouldn't light,
A window rattling
All night,

The lady next door
With the all-night voice,
A rusty razor,
A copy of Joyce,
Corners crowded
With dust and Art
And me alone
With a brand-new heart.

Harrison Dowd

The Rueful Rhyme of a Robin

Does he know that his forefathers, back unto Adam,
    Shouted the same, free tune?
Does he know that when highways were neither macadam,
    Nor ancestors ate with a spoon,
        That his trills were planned,
        As the stars were spanned,
    And the path of the young May moon?

Does he know that his family were singing in Devon
    When Arthur was ruling the Isle?
Does he know that Sir Launcelot was groping for heaven,
    And losing his honor the while,
        When robins were crying,
        And mating and dying,
    And Guinevere wept with a smile?

Does he know that the saxophone (lately invented),
　　Is melody's final word?
Does he care? Does it make him the least discontented
　　With being a One-Tune Bird?
　　　　No—the pompous, old ass
　　　　Struts around on the grass
　　Believing himself still heard!

Patience Eden

In Nature's Garden

Let's to the meadows, lad; the year's at flood,
And the boon earth persuades the errant foot;
Now the shy bugbane carpets all the wood,
And butterflies kiss their darling pleurisy root.
And now the world's green smock is gaily smutch'd
With corpse-plant and with foetid camomile,
And nods the jocund pig-sty daisy, which we'd
　　Best leave untouch'd,
Together with the too-fair-seeming itchweed,
That lures the trustful kine with treach'rous smile.

Unhappy kine, that find amid their fodder
Clammy azalea, or rank scorpion grass!
Sweeter the strangleweed or common dodder
(Or love vine). But away! Away! Let's pass
To brighter meads, where wanton louseworts lodge.
Nosebleed and hairy vetch are thick along
Our dancing way, where none shall see us go
　　Save simple Hodge,
Who for a wondering moment stays his hoe,
And, open-mouth'd, forgets his country song.

Morris Bishop

Woman Out of Taxi

Any woman
   When she's grown
And goes to parties
   All alone

Finds taxicabs
   Exert a spell
That segregate her
   Like a shell

Wherein detached
   From life she's whirled
Through this exciting
   Clamorous world.

Within a cab
   She grows compact,
A separate, keen,
   Dynamic fact,

Unentertained,
   Untouched, unspent,
Safe in her own
   Integument.

Out of the taxi
   She will come
From an emotional
   Vacuum,

Out of the darkness
   Into the light,
As highly charged
   As dynamite.

She draws her cloak
  About her hips,
Twists her bracelet,
  Bites her lips,

From head to toe
  Grows tense and narrow,
Simple and dangerous
  As an arrow

Aimed at a door
  That may, by chance,
Swing inward, brightly,
  On romance.

Angela Cypher

In This Year of Rotogravure

Girl in inset, lithe and limber,
Picked for daisy-chain-girl timber.
Stanford co-eds snapped in poses
For their carnival of roses.
Upper-left-hand picture, readers,
Shows the Smith field-hockey leaders.
Pipe the Holyoke freshmen, would you?
Couldn't sneeze at them, now, could you?
Wellesley campus cleared of brambles
For the barefoot Grecian gambols.
Barnard sophomores are oh so
Keen to stage "Il Penseroso."
Goucher girl from Kansas City
Heads the Senior Prom Committee.
Gaze on Radcliffe's queen of archers,
Gaze on sundry pageant marchers.

Spring is here, and all the papers
Teem with college maidens' capers.

Parke Cummings

Ballad for One Born in Missouri

James Truslow Adams Hopeful—
Sails for England.—*Headline in the Sun.*

Rise up, devout America! The blessed hours strike.
Rise up, rise up, Republicans and Democrats alike.
For Summer is icumen in to meadow, field, and slope.
And James
Truslow
Adams
Is burgeoning with Hope.

> *Pack up your troubles*
>   *And sing in your shower.*
> *The Senate's in session*
>   *And Borah's in flower.*
> *They're jailing a tailor*
>   *For passive resistance,*
> *But James Truslow Adams*
>   *Sees Hope in the distance.*

They've torn apart the alphabet; they're running through the
  "Z"s,
And Revolution rends the ranks that once were Tammany's,
While Freedom from her mountain height leans down to see
  the fun.
But James
Truslow
Adams
Is Hoping for the Sun.

> *Let's deck us with vine leaves*
>   *And dance down the road,*
> *The snail's on the thorn*
>   *And the thorn's in the Code.*

126

For Farley's the postman;
Let no man begrudge it.
And God's in His Heaven
Adjusting the Budget.

The Ship of State has listed but it rights itself once more.
Now timidly Prosperity seeks out her native shore,
And Capital grows proud again and Labor whets her tool.
But James
Truslow
Adams
Sets sail for Liverpool.

Phyllis McGinley

Spring Comes to Murray Hill

I sit in an office at 244 Madison Avenue
And say to myself you have a responsible job, havenue?
Why then do you fritter away your time on this doggerel?
If you have a sore throat you can cure it by using a good
     goggeral,
If you have a sore foot you can get it fixed by a chiropodist
And you can get your original sin removed by St. John the
     Bopodist,
Why then should this flocculent lassitude be incurable?
Kansas City, Kansas, proves that even Kansas City needn't
     always be Missourible.
Up up my soul! This inaction is abominable.
Perhaps it is the result of disturbances abdominable.
The pilgrims settled Massachusetts in 1620 when they landed on
     a stone hummock.
Maybe if they were here now they would settle my stomach.
Oh, if I only had the wings of a bird
Instead of being confined on Madison Avenue I could soar in a
     jiffy to Second or Third.

Ogden Nash

127

I Paint What I See

[A BALLAD OF ARTISTIC INTEGRITY]

"What do you paint, when you paint on a wall?"
  Said John D.'s grandson Nelson.
"Do you paint just anything there at all?
"Will there be any doves, or a tree in fall?
"Or a hunting scene, like an English hall?"

  "I paint what I see," said Rivera.

"What are the colors you use when you paint?"
  Said John D.'s grandson Nelson.
"Do you use any red in the beard of a saint?
"If you do, is it terribly red, or faint?
"Do you use any blue? Is it Prussian?"

  "I paint what I paint," said Rivera.

"Whose is that head that I see on my wall?"
  Said John D.'s grandson Nelson.
"Is it anyone's head whom we know, at all?
"A Rensselaer, or a Saltonstall?
"Is it Franklin D.? Is it Mordaunt Hall?
"Or is it the head of a Russian?"

  "I paint what I think," said Rivera.

  "I paint what I paint, I paint what I see,
    "I paint what I think," said Rivera,
  "And the thing that is dearest in life to me
  "In a bourgeois hall is Integrity;
    "However . . .
  "I'll take out a couple of people drinkin'
  "And put in a picture of Abraham Lincoln;

128

"I could even give you McCormick's reaper
"And still not make my art much cheaper.
"But the head of Lenin has got to stay
"Or my friends will give me the bird today,
    "The bird, the bird, forever."

"It's not good taste in a man like me,"
    Said John D.'s grandson Nelson,
"To question an artist's integrity
"Or mention a practical thing like a fee,
"But I know what I like to a large degree,
    "Though art I hate to hamper;
"For twenty-one thousand conservative bucks
"You painted a radical. I say shucks,
    "I never could rent the offices—
    "The capitalistic offices.
"For this, as you know, is a public hall
"And people want doves, or a tree in fall,
"And though your art I dislike to hamper,
"I owe a *little* to God and Gramper,
    "And after all,
    "It's *my* wall . . ."

    "We'll see if it is," said Rivera.
                            E. B. White

Warning

When the universe began
God, they say, created man.

Later, with a mocking nod,
Man annihilated God.
Watch your worlds, or they may do
Something of the kind to you.
                        Miriam Vedder

129

Elegy for Janes

Historical fact: "All female rulers named Jane were murdered, became insane, or were deposed."—*From "Believe It Or Not."*

Light a taper,
Say a prayer
A bluish vapour
In holy air,
    For poor Queen Jane.

Queens named Jane
Go insane.
Fire and stone
For Queens named Joan,
Jehan and Jeanne
Die scorned by man.

This gentle name
Brings a curse,
Draggled fame,
Hanging—worse,
Murder, rack-pains,
Madness, flight,
Fret and hack Janes

Day and night.
A royal flitter,
She knows no ease.
Life's drink is bitter
To its very lees.

Speed her reign
She had a tryst,
Cursèd Jane
With an alienist,
A burly traitor,

A guillotine,
Run by a satyr,
Life treats her mean.

Death's a gain
Bringing release.
May Queens named Jane
Rest In Peace.

Rosemary Carr Benét

Résumé

Though kings go grandly under the arch
Whose pillars stand in the night;
Whose pillars stand in the night, whose base
Is the dust that once was might;

Though kings go under in gold and scarlet,
And the bishop in broidered cope,
And the tall archangels blow their trumpets
To hail the returning pope;

I would go under without a whisper,
Under the arch of Death,
Like quiet water that flows in darkness
In air that holds its breath;

Incurious of all that is or *may* be;
Incurious of glory or God,
Like ashes settling, or dead leaves falling
Silently on the sod.

For I've had enough of wanting and fretting,
Enough of having and grief,
As all the summers that ever *will* be
Fall in a falling leaf.

Samuel Hoffenstein

Plans for a Horrid Old Age

When I am old and vastly rich
I'll join a Club. I don't know which,
But it must be
The very *ne*
Plus ultra of society.
It ought to have a holy hush
And chairs upholstered in red plush.

I'll breakfast at precisely ten-
Fourteen each day. And always when
The waiter brings my steak
I'll make
A hue and cry and have him take
It back and notify the cook
'Twas too well done, or raw. I'll look
For dirt upon the silverware
And find it, whether it is there
Or not.
I'll always order what
The menu shows they haven't got;
I'll rant because the tea's too hot;
I'll charge the steward with a plot
To poison me. And when I'm stuffed
And gorged and puffed,
Like some old toad too full of flies
To blink his bulging, glassy eyes,
I'll totter to the window where
They've placed my chair—
My private chair—
And there
I'll sit and glare
At passers-by in the thoroughfare.

When I am bored with that, I'll call
A bell-boy—no, I'll get them all,

The whole damn crew,
To page me for an hour or two.

All day I'll growl and grouch and grouse
And mutter curses on the House
Committee, for no other reason
Than that it is the grousing season
(Which lasts from early in December
Till late the following November).

And all I'll think about will be
Me.

John Ogden Whedon

Midnight Sailing

I tell myself and I tell myself
  It's only a ferryboat whistling loud;
I tell myself it's only a tug
  That blows so deep and toots so proud.

I scrunch way down in the foot of my bed
  In a house too plainly anchored to earth.
There isn't a porthole over my head
  And I tell myself I'm not in a berth.

You can't hear taxis squeak their brakes
  Where a sharp prow cuts the waves in two,
And sailors never make the noise
  That early-morning milkmen do.

I tell myself and I tell myself
  I'm lucky to have the rent this week—
But the chair in the corner answers me
  With the whine of a tarry halyard's creak.

Elspeth

133

Californiana

Getting acclimated, I find,
Requires a stoic state of mind.
Unpleasant weather here denotes
"A most unusual year"—in quotes.
That's how the Native Sons explain
A solid week of sluicing rain.
And when the Santa Ana blows
Dust in your teeth and up your nose,
Why, people caution you it's quite
Exceptional—they must be right.
Umbrellas and galoshes cause
Arched eyebrows and the awkward pause,
As though one actually defied
The sanctity of Civic Pride.
And as for overcoats, they treat
Such cosiness as most effete,
Fit only for that bloodless drone
Who tolerates the Frigid Zone.
Then there's the sun—perpetual boast
Of everybody on the Coast.
It shines and shines with a serene
Indifference to a Golden Mean,
Which simple souls prefer instead
Of aching eyes and burning head.
No doubt the Chamber of Commerce knows
Why deserts burgeon like the rose,
How palms and cacti and the scent
Of orange blossoms bring content.
It's all The Climate—with a due
Regard to irrigation, too.
But what is April in a land
That runs eternally to sand?
Little they guess what happens when
The last thaw heralds spring again

And green fire tips the willow wands,
And a thin music shakes the ponds!
Somewhere the dogwood will resume
Its frail, white ritual of bloom;
And up Westchester way there'll be
Red tufts on many a maple tree.
Getting acclimated. . . . Ah, well,
They're shivering still in New Rochelle!

Leslie Nelson Jennings

Telephonetics

What lyric artisan arranges
The names of telephone exchanges?
How tunefully their accents ring:
"Algonquin, Pennsylvania, Spring,
Bogardus, Chelsea, Audubon,
Trafalgar, Orchard, Plaza, John."
In all the records of Euphonia
What sweeter call than "Caledonia"?
And where a softer madrigal
Than "Mohawk, Butterfield, Canal"?
"Cathedral" rises like a prayer-word
And "Sacramento!" like a swear-word;
And as the laughing, rippling rill
Are "Riverside" and "Murray Hill."
By Pegasus, the poets' stallion,
No word is grander than "Medallion"!
And be there blither songs of earth
Than "Eldorado, Lehigh, Worth"?
Then gaily carol: "Lackawanna,
Columbus, Bryant, Susquehanna;"
Or lift the sounding martial chant:
"Lorraine, Wisconsin, Stuyvesant!"

Arthur Guiterman

135

To a Small Boy Standing on My Shoes While I Am Wearing Them

Let's straighten this out, my little man,
And reach an agreement if we can.
I entered your door as an honored guest.
My shoes are shined and my trousers are pressed,
And I won't stretch out and read you the funnies
And I won't pretend that we're Easter bunnies.
If you must get somebody down on the floor,
What in the hell are your parents for?
I do not like the things that you say
And I hate the games that you want to play.
No matter how frightfully hard you try,
We've little in common, you and I.
The interest I take in my neighbor's nursery
Would have to grow to be even cursory,
And I would that performing sons and nephews
Were carted away with the daily refuse,
And I hold that frolicsome daughters and nieces
Are ample excuse for breaking leases.
You may take a sock at your daddy's tummy
Or climb all over your doting mummy,
But keep your attentions to me in check
Or, sonny boy, I will wring your neck.
A happier man today I'd be
Had a visiting adult done it to me.

Ogden Nash

The Thinker

I think of such absorbing things
   As I go walking down the street.
I think how water snakes have died
   To decorate my pointed feet.

I think how I have set to work
   The iron wheels of industry,

I think how frazzled silkworms toil
  That I may have pink lingerie.

For me the goldsmith learns his craft,
  For me the ox and lamb have bled,
For me the silver wheat goes down
  To fill my crying mouth with bread;

And seven little jungle cats
  Laid down their lives the other day
That I might have a stripèd coat,
  So you would cock one eye my way.
                              Persis Greely Anderson

The Involuntary Collector

I keep a fairly expensive flat
And what, after all, do I gain by that?

I keep good Scotch and three-star brandy,
Caviar and nice, fresh candy,

A silent Jap in a spotless coat,
Tropical fish that fight and float,

And furniture made out of tubes and tin.
What does all of this bring me in?

Bobby-pins, compacts, rouge-stained rags,
Lipsticks, Bobby-pins, beaded bags,

Gloves all sizes, lengths, and skins,
And Bobby-pins, Bobby-pins, Bobby-pins.

If they've got to leave them around my flat,
For God's sake why must they call them that?
                              Jake Falstaff

Tu Ne Quaesieris

(Horace I. 11)

The night rolled out like velvet
And we drove from inn to inn.
And we drank a little purple wine,
We drank a little gin,
And I leaned my sight against your eyes
And saw what lay within.

Tu ne quaesieris (scire nefas)

We sat at ivory tables
And we played with amber ale.
The air grew warm and heavy
The cigarettes burned stale.
The saxophone drew through the night
A deep barbaric trail.

                    quem mihi, quem tibi
Finem di dederint, Leuconoe,

Then moaned the saxophone, then crooned the coon:
Why don't you try these swoonin' blues
Take a chance
On a trance
Your girl's a dancing fool.

                    nec Babylonios
Temptaris numeros.

We crossed the long verandah
And found the swaying door.
The peril streamed through us like flags.
We waved across the floor.
Although we both were silent
We heard a steady roar.

Swoon as the coon advises,
Lean as he tantalizes,
Swing with the swinging violin,
Faint with the wine and gin
Against me. Lay your ear
Upon me. Hear the roar and din.

Ut melius quidquid erit pati!
Seu plures hiemes seu tribuit Juppiter ultimam,

If day should end at evening, and night be spent alone—
But listen to the colored man moan and groan.
But listen to the banjo and the saxophone.
Night was made to keep the flesh
From thinking of the bone.
Night was never made for those
Who have to lie alone:
Rock and sway
Take a chance on a trance
This girl's a dancing fool.

Close your ear to the shoring surge that tides upon the heart.
It ebbed and flowed before you came, it will roar when you
   depart.
It's naught to do with love or gin, and naught with nigger's
   groan.
It is the flesh remembering that it's briefer than the bone.

Quae nunc oppositis debilitat pumicibus mare
Tyrrhenum;

Tomorrow all will clear away before a clear cold light,
If this girl is any lady she will quite forget tonight.

sapias, vina liques et spatio brevi
Spem longam reseces!

The night rolls out like velvet
Yet here we sit and wait.
It's all been said a thousand years
About the ways of fate.
The night rolls out like velvet
And it's growing very late.

Dum loquimur, fugerit invida
Aetas; carpe diem,

Listen to the banjo and the saxophone.
Listen to the colored man moan and groan:
Night was never made for those
Who have to lie alone.
Night was made to keep the flesh
From remembering the bone.

quam minimum credula postero.

Clinch Calkins

Spring

Spring is largely overrated
When one is already mated.

Myra M. Waterman

VI. JUNE: *At summer's brink*

A General Survey of Early Summer
in Town and Country

Oh, here we sit at summer's brink,
  With art and music at a standstill,
    So hail the clink
    Of sidewalk drink,
  And Junish weather seeming grand still.

In Summit, Stockbridge, Dennis (Mass.),
  The little-theatre groups assemble;
    Bright chiffons pass
    In the cool grass,
  And newborn actors all a-tremble.

In town, the drama groweth lean,
  An intimate and somewhat coarse show.
    Smart folks are seen
    On Armonk's green
  When Jack & Charlie stage a horse show.

At Greenwich depot and at Rye
  Descends at eve the homing broker;
    His wife sits by
    With welcoming eye
  In sport coupé of yellow ochre.

Observe the scene through country gates,
  The North Shore section, for example:
    Charity fêtes
    On large estates,
  And beds of foxglove deep in trample,

Where matrons vaunt the garden's crop,
  And débutantes the summer knees,
    And Scouts pick up
    The Lily cup,
  And men get sick in back of trees.

Sky-blue the stands of Meadow Brook
  O'er Hitchcock (Tom) and Cowdin (Cheever).
    The subway's nook
    Betrays the look
  Of those who suffer from hay fever.

Now Mrs. Stanwood Menken haunts
  The shingle of her favorite beach club,
    Yet nothing daunts
    The crowd that wants
  The middle-class, not-hard-to-reach club.

Oh, fierce the highway's gaseous deck,
  The Sunday traveler returning;
    The steaming check
    Of bottleneck,
  And idle engine idly churning.

Apartment life grows unafraid
  For those whom heat has got a grip on,
    And pretty maid
    With undrawn shade
  Doth loll about with just her slip on.

So wind the merry hunting horn
  O'er penthouse roof and dale a-blooming,
    Dewy the thorn
    In park at morn—
  The swan-boat trade again is booming.

And pause with me at summer's brink;
   The days are long, the nights are stifling;
     All hail the clink
     Of sidewalk drink:
Life is a glorious show, though trifling.
E. B. White

Refrain from the Palisades

I want to be a Yosian, and go and take a walk,
I want to eat a hard-boiled egg and hear a Nature Talk;
I want to join a Bird Group, and go without a hat,
And peer at ants and cherish plants and carry on like that,
And when I'm grown, revered of all—aunt, uncle, parent, cousin,
I'll be the sort of chap, you know, who does the Daily Dozen.
Sylvia Fuller

Boston Baby

   Selma went to the Winsor School,
   Bryn Mawr College, her Ultima Thule.
   She took her junior year abroad,
   Adopted "Sapristi" and dropped "Migawd."
   Selma belongs to the Vincent Club.
   She never bathes, she takes a tub.
   Selma summers in Lancaster South.
   Selma's laugh never reaches her mouth.
   She's a love on water-color trips,
   Her best gouache was the last eclipse.
   Selma's posture shows she fences.
   She unbends at Consequences.
   Her conception of the pace that kills
   Is a *tour d'Espagne* in espadrilles.
   Born not for toil in life's colosseum,
   She works for fun in the Fogg Museum.
Katherine Curtis Sappington

The Man Behind the Buttons

O passer-by, beware the lean,
Austere patrolman. He is mean
And crabbed in his view of life.
He uses oaths, he beats his wife,
He frightens children in the street,
He robs the fruit carts on his beat,
He sneers at Lindbergh, yes he does,
He doesn't know who Lincoln was
Or even care. To save his skin
He'd gladly see a friend run in.

From life he has distilled this crass
Philosophy: "Keep off the grass!"
The letter is the law to him,
The spirit contraband. And slim
The chance of anyone who dares
Deride the Force whose shield he wears.
His heaven is a one-way street
With fire-plugs every twenty feet,
And God a dick so skilled in craft
No higher-up can split His graft.

But fat patrolmen, you will find,
Are philosophical and kind.
They watch the world, from day to day,
Go by, and speed it on its way
With now a red, and now a green,
And now a sock upon the bean.

While Progress, with its clanking wheels,
Rolls past, they rock upon their heels
And solve, for those inclined to hear,
The riddles of our tangled sphere.
Their slogan, in this vale of sorrow,
Is "Here today and gone tomorrow."

                    John Ogden Whedon

Bull Hill

A news item announces the sale of Mount Taurus, the fourteen-hundred-foot mountain on the Hudson opposite the Storm King Highway, to a company which plans to quarry granite from it. If the quarrying operations are allowed at this point, the scenery will be permanently marred.

Dirk Van Tull had a roaring bull,
A big, black, bellowing, Bashan bull
With short, hard horns on a massive head,
Small eyes that gleamed a cruel red,
Defiant hooves, a tasselled tail
That smote his flanks like a thresher's flail,
A brawny neck and a dewlapped throat
That rent the sky with its martial note.
You couldn't gentle, drive, or lead him,
Nor water, curry, bed, or feed him;
He went his way and lived at ease
While people ran and climbed up trees
When they heard the challenge, deep and full,
Of the big, black, bellowing, Bashan bull.

The sun had set in Ramapo
And mirror-smooth was Hudson's flow
When on Bear Mountain's rugged form
And all the Highlands burst the storm.
From every peak the thunder spoke;
From dreams of war the bull awoke,
Red anger thrilling every limb—
The bellowing mountains challenged *him!*
In trampling rage he spurned the stall,
He crashed the door, he leaped the wall;
Straight up the mountain tore the bull
While hard behind came Dirk Van Tull.

The great bull stamped upon the crest;
The thunder rolled from old Cro' Nest.
The great bull roared, and far and wide
The roar of Dunderberg replied.
The great bull blared his answer back,
And shouting through the cloudy wrack
Where lightning played in vivid jags
The voice of Storm King shook the crags.
The great bull pawed the flinty shelf
And raged like Lucifer himself;
From brazen throat and foaming mouth
He bellowed north and west and south.

But while, belligerently proud,
He hurled his wrath to crag and cloud
Like Ajax, challenging the thunder,
The hill beneath him split asunder!
In vain his master pulled his tail;
What could such feeble force avail?
Away, away from Dirk Van Tull
Right down the chasm plunged the bull,
When, yielding to the earthquake shock,
Around him closed the living rock.
So, prisoned in the mighty hill,
He vents his fury, bellowing still.

For still when sullen thunders grumble
You hear the great bull's muffled rumble;
And when you call his mountain "Taurus"
He bellows like a brontosaurus.
Then hark, you vandals—you that trouble
Our cliffs and grind our hills to rubble,
Profaning all with shaft and quarry—
Touch not this hill, or you'll be sorry!
Blast not this citadel, forbear
To cleave its wall—the bull is there!
And if you break his prison door,
Where shall you flee when, roar on roar,

A prodigy of strength immortal,
He charges through the shattered portal?
For other horns are soft as wool
Compared with those of Bull Hill's bull!

Arthur Guiterman

Coney Island

Go to Coney Island where the bright lights twinkle,
  City warm and playful with a hard gold soul;
    Take your dinner early
    While the sky's still pearly,
Have a lot of change to tinkle,
  And a fat bank roll.

Lay aside the languor of your safe sane marriage,
  Never mind the people whom your own set snubs,
    Shelve your inhibishes,
    Free your half-starved wishes,
And forget your haughty carriage
  And your five best clubs.

Ride a roller coaster for a good night's starter;
  Pinch her on the kneecap if your girl won't go;
    Throw her down the slideways
    Till her hat's on sideways
And the ruffles on her garter
  Make a nice bright show.

Europe, Asia, Africa have mild wild places,
  Even Greeks and Romans had their own rough fun;
    But Coney on this globule
    Has the real live mob—you'll
See a half a million faces
  And you won't know one.

Fillmore Hyde

Knockout

MADISON SQUARE GARDEN

When he fell,
All heard the thud
And a cold bell
Ring in their blood.

Upon his back,
Upon the floor,
The world went black
And like a roar.

The referee
Began to swing;
He could not see
The lighted ring,
The referee
Or anything.

The people rose
To see him lying
Like a man dead
Or a man dying.

His mouth bled
Until the gore
Burned like a red
Rose on the floor.

The lights glowed,
The air rang,
And through it flowed
The bell's clang.

Charles Norman

150

Kitten in a Graveyard

You pick your way among the dead
With padded and fastidious tread,
Your tail so high, your fur so sleek;
You are the strong and I the weak
Who fear this quiet spot of serried
Tombs where everything is buried
Except the evergreen and stone
For you to whet your claws upon.
I ask to live, if only that
I may be here to stroke you, cat.

Selma Robinson

Truce

By these you may know the young: by the unsteady breath,
  By eyes enlarged with tears for love's fallow season,
  By the flowers they wear that had no root in reason,
But chiefly by their feud with time and death.

Youth's heart is hot as it were a phoenix nest,
  With burning plumage from whose ashes rising
  Are joys and terrors past the sober mind's devising,
But terror of time flames fiercer than the rest.

Youth being done, the heart learns how to bear
  The confronted darkness: never the sun's bright legions
  Are called to succor those in polar regions
Whom night that lasts a winter cannot scare.

Youth being done, the tears and the burning are slaked.
  Small memorial rests of the feud that was so savage.
  For look, there is no more for time to ravage,
And truce is sworn, on the field that death has raked.

Babette Deutsch

Morbid Reflections

I

The gonad is designed to mate us,
And thereby, obviously, create us,
Whereas the mute, minute bacillus
Is admirably made to kill us:
A balanced budget in this case
Would greatly benefit the race.

II

The weirdest ills are put to rout
By having teeth and tonsils out,
But if, with teeth and tonsils banished,
The ills referred to have not vanished,
It is generally understood
The operations did no good.

III

An ostrich on his native sand
Is worth a couple in the hand;
The same is applicable to
The minatory marabou,
Although the proverb may insist
A bird is worth more in the fist.

IV

Women have three years to hope in;
The fourth, they leap into the open,
And hence, by masculine acclaim,
Leap year gets its name and fame,
Although, with subtle skill in mating,
They pull some fast ones, too, while waiting.

V

The oceans, like necrophilists,
Paw dead shores and breed dead mists;
The mineral eyes of darkness stare
As blind as bats on barren air—
Thus do the seas and stars equip
The studious mind for statesmanship.

VI

A craven fellow, I abhor
The fierce phenomena of war:
The sudden shell, the constant stench,
The frigid steel, the flooded trench—
Half-enviously, I declare
Only the brave deserve such fare.

VII

Minnows live in shady ponds;
Bankers live in shady bonds;
Illusions, when the blossoms fall,
Live on a dole in alcohol;
Most of us live, with troubled breath,
In hope of dying a painless death.

Samuel Hoffenstein

Tradition

Where'd be song
And where'd be story
If some love
Weren't desultory?

Ruth Lambert Jones

Problems for an Analyst

Can you decipher, point by point,
The delicately angled joint
Of a beloved wrist whereon
You set a swift, impulsive kiss?
Can you unravel moments gone
And label them as this and this . . .
Coldly, and with no sense of loss?
In ravaging the healing moss
About the spring's long-thirsty bed,
Do you say earth was scarcely fed
And men were poorly quenched by cool
Water in a shadowed pool;
Or do you stand aside and only
Mark that men and springs may die
From seeing little of the sky,
Being intrinsically lonely?

Frances Frost

Prelude

Music will more nimbly move
than quick wit can order word;
words can point or speaking prove
but music heard

How with successions it can take
time in change and change in time
and all reorder, all remake,
with no recourse to rhyme!

Let us in joy, let us in love,
surrender speech to music, tell
what music so much more can prove
nor talking say so well:

Love with delight may move away
love with delight may forward come
or else will hesitate and stay
finger at lip, at home;

but verse can never say these things;
only in music may be heard
the subtle touching of such strings,
never in word.

Conrad Aiken

Prelude

Not with the noting of a private hate,
as if one put a mark down in a book;
nor with the chronicling of a private love,
as if one cut a vein and let it bleed;
nor the observing of peculiar light,
nor the remembrance of a singular phrase
ringed round with what refractions peace can bring—
give it up, phrase-maker! Your note is nothing.
The sum is everything.

Who walks attended by delight will feel it,
whom sudden sorrow hushes, he will know.
But you, who mark the drooping of an eyelid,
or in a wrinkled cheek set out a reason—
you too are sainted; but only if you see—
                              ah yes, and only then—
why, that the sum of all your notes is nothing.
Make a rich note of this. And start again.

Conrad Aiken

A Father Does His Best

Said I to Lord & Taylor:
  "Hot are the summer skies,
  And my son Joe would like to go
  In a big straw hat in the year-old size.
  Have you got such a thing, for summer skies,
  A nice straw hat in the year-old size?"
Said Lord & Taylor: "No."

Said I to Saks Fifth Avenue:
  "The sunshine hurts Joe's eyes;
  He used to nap in a small white cap,
  But a big straw hat in the year-old size
  Would keep the sunshine out of his eyes.
  Have you got such a thing in the year-old size?"
Said Saks Fifth Avenue: "No."

Said I to Best & Company:
  "I think it might be wise
  When noons are red to cover Joe's head
  With a big straw hat in the year-old size.
  Can you sell me one, if you think it's wise,
  A big straw hat in the year-old size?"
Said Best & Company: "No."

Said I to the infant's mother:
  "It comes as a great surprise
  That our son Joe may never go
  In a big straw hat in the year-old size.
  We had no trouble with his other supplies,
  His Pyrex bottles, his spoon for eating,
  His year-old pot and his year-old sheeting,
  His feeding bib of heavy material
  To catch the spray from the flying cereal,

Rompers to match the color of his eyes
    In the year-old size;
These things were bought with the greatest ease,
The stores were willing and able to please,
His bands and his year-old shirts all fit,
His crew-neck sweater and his Arnold-Knit,
I bought him a bear and a rubber cat,
Yet now, when he needs a big straw hat,
    I don't know where to go.
Doesn't it come as a great surprise
That there's no straw hat in the year-old size
    To keep the sun from the little lad's eyes?"
Said the infant's mother: "No."

                                        E. B. White

Belle Isle

When the fog lifted and the little steamer
Jangled her bells and shivered and went on,
We all ran to the rail, as the redeemer
Examines the watch he's taken out of pawn.
The sea was flat and pallid, not as we left it,
And rising to the north we saw Belle Isle
And twenty-five green icebergs which had drifted
Down the cold Labrador in timeless trial.
We thought "How noble," but we said "How thrilling,"
And five or six diminished in our lens;
One was a tile-square block, as if the willing
Iceman had dropped it in and shaved the ends.
We watched a great show, and some faces set there
For slow oblivion in the souther suns;
The seals rose in the still sea, and we were met there
By white gulls and the grayer young and those other ones.
We heard the lookout repeat the hour, saw the ranks
Break with the lost freighter whistling on the Banks.

                                        David McCord

Excavations in Ur

I

And that Sumerian Queen, the powdered gold
Upon her hair, the golden ribbon coiled
Intricately, the lapis frontlet foiled
With gold shell, and the wreath of willow scrolled
With flowers of gold, and the gold rings that rolled
Whenever she shook her little lovely spoiled
Impertinent head, and one more dark throat soiled
A sword or axe—even that Queen is mold.

Even Shub-Ad is nothing; but her two
Gold fish and two gold antelopes and beads
Of the carnelian and the lapis blue
Survive their mistress: metal never bleeds—
Only the heart that not again shall mark
Her golden earrings jingling in the dark.

II

Your black hair stains the darkness as one flame
Might drown another; black pearls are your eyes;
Your mouth is small and dangerously wise;
Your breasts are little torches making shame
As sweet as flowers with a fiery name;
Your hands are light as lilies; golden flies
Dart in your fingers; golden tiny lies
Dance in your words and weave a praise of blame.

And yet there was a lovely queen in Ur,
Even the Queen Shub-Ad: and on her head
Clustered gold mulberry leaves. . . . And I am sure
That she was beautiful, that she is dead,
And that her dust is fragrant, and that your
Fragrance is dust and dust the words we said.

Joseph Auslander

158

The Proud

And though we need not stoop to pick a penny,
    Let us walk humbly on this street.
Where enemies are proud and many,
    Let us be pale and simulate defeat.

For then they will have done with us and talking,
    And we can walk on any street we will,
Where half the city's people may be walking,
    And none to wish us ill.

Charles Norman

Susanna Passes

Harden not your hearts,
You with whom the wise
Sit as counsellors;
Narrow not your eyes

When she walks your street
With her band of fools
Whose exultant feet,
Dancing, make your rules

Words of no account,
Formulas outgrown—
If she ask for bread,
Will you give a stone?

Furtive whispers pass,
Lips and eyes are set.
Shall this golden bird
Tremble in your net?

In your hearts contempt
Sets a knell to ringing;
She will heed you not,
She will pass you singing.
                    Sydney King Russell

The Cup of Day

The revolutions of the night,
    The planets' subtle roll,
The spirals of the stars unwind
    My morning-glory's scroll.

The high, whole night is over me,
    Earth's shadow rears away,
Yet this tight and fluted cup
    Is full of busy day.

I shall not be so early up
    To see the east turn gold,
But there will be a little heaven
    Before my eyes unrolled.
                    Robert P. Tristram Coffin

Song for the Nearest Riveting Machine

Life is a con game, life is a flop,
Life is a cloud that grows darker and darker.
Trouble and worry and work till you drop,
Life is a poem by Dorothy Parker.

What does it get you to hustle and slave?
A nice grassy plot with a white marble marker.
Out of the cradle and into the grave—
Life is a poem by Dorothy Parker.

Life is a swindle and life is a gyp,
Life is a shell game, and Death is the barker.
Spring always gives me a touch of the pip,
And life is a poem by Dorothy Parker.
Newman Levy

Summing Up

I do not know what Mr. Darrow is trying to say. . . . It sounds like
a proposal to have white blackbirds, flying cats, and whales that walk.
—*Walter Lippmann on the Darrow Report on the NRA.*

Snowy blackbirds, flying cats,
Whales that walk, and feathered rats,
Mewing dogs, and barking birds,
Lowing doves, and cooing herds,
Walter Lippmann boop-a-dooping,
Helen Kane consigned to snooping
In the field of politics. . . .
There would be a bag of tricks.
Margaret Fishback

This Is My House . . .

This is my house, where everything lives in its space and its story,
Everything is worn smooth with touch and with time—
The linens are soft and the chairs have hollows in them,
Every tool fits my hand.
There is no place in my house that is not used and familiar.
I can walk in the dark here.

I have made my house clean:
The brass sticks are thin in their saucers
From many scourings of sand,
And sheets were bleached the week the pear tree bloomed.
The windows show only for having
Here a pane of the color of water,

There one like a glass rinsed with wine;
The windows are barred by clear-starched Swiss,
But I have touched to the door latch a feather dipped in oil.

Harriett Brownell

To a Lady, Who Must Write Verse

Unto seventy years and seven,
  Hide your double birthright well—
You, that are the brat of heaven,
  And the pampered heir to hell.

Let your rhymes be tinsel treasures,
  Strung and seen and thrown aside.
Drill your apt and docile measures
  Sternly as you drill your pride.

Show your quick, alarming skill in
  Tidy mockeries of art.
Never, never dip your quill in
  Ink that trickles from your heart.

When your pain must come to paper,
  See it dust, before the day;
Let your night-light curl and caper—
  Let it lick the words away.

Never print, poor child, a lay on
  Love and blood and anguishing,
Lest a cooled, benignant Phaon
  Murmur, "Foolish little thing!"

Dorothy Parker

VII. JULY: *Music on the Mall*

Metropolitan Nightmare

It rained quite a lot, that spring. You woke in the morning
And saw the sky still clouded, the streets still wet,
But nobody noticed so much, except the taxis
And the people who parade. You don't, in a city.
The parks got very green. All the trees were green
Far into July and August, heavy with leaf,
Heavy with leaf and the long roots boring and spreading,
But nobody noticed that but the city gardeners,
And they don't talk.
     Oh, on Sundays perhaps, you'd notice:
Walking through certain blocks, by the shut, proud houses
With the windows boarded, the people gone away,
You'd suddenly seen the queerest small shoots of green
Poking through cracks and crevices in the stone
And a bird-sown flower, red on a balcony,
But then you made jokes about grass growing in the streets
And the end of the depression—and there were songs
And gags and a musical show called "Hot and Wet."
It all made a good box for the papers. When the flamingo
Flew into a meeting of the Board of Estimate,
Mayor O'Brien acted at once and called the photographers.
When the first green creeper crawled upon Brooklyn Bridge,
They thought it was ornamental. They let it stay.

That was the year the termites came to New York
And they don't do well in cold climates—but listen, Joe,
They're only ants and ants are nothing but insects.
It was funny and yet rather wistful, in a way
(As Heywood Broun pointed out in the *World-Telegram*),
To think of them looking for wood in a steel city.
It made you feel about life. It was too divine.
There were funny pictures by Steig and Peter Arno
And Macy's ran a terribly clever ad:
"The Widow's Termite" or something.

There was no
Disturbance. Even the Communists didn't protest
And say they were Morgan hirelings. It was too hot,
Too hot to protest, too hot to get excited,
An even, African heat, lush, fertile, and steamy,
That soaked into bone and mind and never once broke.
The warm rain fell in fierce showers and ceased and fell.
Pretty soon you got used to its always being that way.

You got used to the changed rhythm, the altered beat,
To people walking slower, to the whole bright
Fierce pulse of the city slowing, to men in shorts,
The new sun helmets from Best's and cops' white uniforms
And the long noon rest in the offices, everywhere.

It wasn't a plan or anything. It just happened.
The fingers tapped the keys slower, the office boys
Dozed on their benches, the bookkeeper yawned at his desk.
The A.T. & T. was the first to change the shifts
And establish an official siesta-room,
But they were always efficient. Mostly it just
Happened like sleep itself, like a tropic sleep,
Till even the Thirties were deserted at noon
Except for a few tourists and one damp cop.
They ran boats to see the lilies on the North River,
But it was only the tourists who really noticed
The flocks of rose-and-green parrots and parrakeets
Nesting in the stone crannies of the Cathedral.
The rest of us had forgotten when they first came.

There wasn't any real change, it was just a heat spell,
A rain spell, a funny summer, a weatherman's joke
In spite of the geraniums three feet high
In the tin-can gardens of Hester and Desbrosses.
New York was New York. It couldn't turn inside out.
When they got the news from Woods Hole about the Gulf
    Stream,

166

The *Times* ran an adequate story,
But nobody reads those stories but science cranks.

Until, one day, a somnolent city editor
Gave a new cub the termite yarn to break his teeth on.
The cub was just down from Vermont, so he took the time.
He was serious about it. He went around.
He read all about termites in the Public Library
And it made him sore when they fired him.

So, one evening,

Talking with an old watchman, beside the first
Raw girders of the new Planetopolis Building
(Ten thousand brine-cooled offices, each with shower),
He saw a dark line creeping across the rubble
And turned a flashlight on it.

"Say, buddy," he said.

"You better look out for those ants. They eat wood, you know.
They'll have your shack down in no time."

The watchman spat.

"Oh, they've quit eating wood," he said, in a casual voice,
"I thought everybody knew that"

—and, reaching down,

He pried from the insect jaws the bright crumb of steel.

Stephen Vincent Benét

Traffic Lights

THIRTY-SECOND STREET AND FIFTH AVENUE

Said the driver of Bus Number Five to the driver of Fifteen:
"A dame was at our house last night, the warmest ever I seen.
Already she's had eight husbands, with boy friends in between,
And the funniest thing about her was—" Here the traffic lights
    turned green.
"See you again sometime," called Five to the driver of Fifteen.

Ellen McLoughlin

167

Century of Progress

[TO A TUNE FROM "IOLANTHE"]

When Washington was President,
A century ago,
Our statesmen didn't advertise
Assorted brands of merchandise
Upon the radio.
And yet we set the world ablaze
In George's grand and glorious days.

CHORUS:

And yet we set the world ablaze
In George's grand and glorious days.

When Lincoln ruled our well-known land
In time of storm and stress,
No piece by Nicolay or Hay
About the questions of the day
Was printed in the press.
Yet Freedom wore her proudest bays
Back in Abe Lincoln's glorious days.

CHORUS:

Yet Freedom wore her proudest bays,
Back in Abe Lincoln's glorious days.

So if our noble master minds
Will keep from actions rash:
Stop advertising soaps and shoes,
And writing comments on the news,
And raking in the cash—
As bright will shine Columbia's rays
As in our country's early days.

   As bright will shine Columbia's rays
   As in our country's early days.
                            Newman Levy

Reflections on Douglas Fairbanks

[AFTER HAVING SEEN HIM IN THE FLESH, AT TAHITI]

Are the teeth, so dazzling white,
Bared in the well-known grin at night?
Does he wear it when alone?
Is it now so much his own
That he cannot, if he would,
Alter it in any mood?

It must be so. A face will bear
Only so much constant wear;
Then it takes a final shape
From which there can be no escape.

Woe to him who is possessed
Of a grin, though of the best!
Friends may die—his nearest kin:
Willy-nilly, he must grin.
Waking, sleeping, drunk or sober,
From October to October,
Without cause, or rhyme, or reason,
In, but mostly out of, season
On his poor abusèd face
Sits the grin he can't erase.

Movie aspirants, beware
How your perfect teeth you bare!
Let his fate a warning be.
Grin, but not eternally.
                            James Norman Hall

Pour Prendre Congé

I'm sick of embarking in dories
  Upon an emotional sea.
I'm wearied of playing Dolores
  (A rôle never written for me).

I'll never again like a cub lick
  My wounds while I squeal at the hurt.
No more I'll go walking in public,
  My heart hanging out of my shirt.

I'm tired of entwining me garlands
  Of weather-worn hemlock and bay.
I'm over my longing for far lands—
  I wouldn't give *that* for Cathay.

I'm through with performing the ballet
  Of love unrequited and told.
Euterpe, I tender you *vale;*
  Good-bye, and take care of that cold.

I'm done with this burning and giving
  And reeling the rhymes of my woes.
And how I'll be making my living,
  The Lord in His mystery knows.

Dorothy Parker

Echo

You
Over there
Beyond the hill
Have nothing to say
Yet can't keep still—
Have nothing to do
But mimic me

And double the words
That I set free.
Garrulous ghost!
Garrulous ghost.

Maybe you'd say
In your defence
No echo practices
Reticence,
And the repartee
Of a voice's ghost
Makes conversation
As good as most!
As good as most.
                    Mildred Weston

The Old Masters

Each sport can boast its king or queen
Whose names with glory glow.
None more than Dr. Alekhine
And Herr Bogoljubow.

Some like to golf or swim or row
Or gambit on the green.
Not so with Herr Bogoliubow
And Dr. Alekhine.

In any sport you've ever seen
The heroes come and go.
Except in chess: it's "Alekhine
To meet Bogoljubow."

Their jangled nerves they never show,
Though competition's keen.
It's *"C'est à vous, Bogoljubow."*
And *"Danke, Alekhine."*

"*C'est votre tour, Bogoljubow.*"
And "*Alekhine, ich danke.*" *
And every other week or so,
"*Si, Señor Capablanca.*"

When gray beards grace the brothers Dean
And Cunningham is slow,
When Tilden passes from the scene
And others steal the show,

When Bobby Jones, with hair of snow,
Is wheeled from green to green,
There'll always be Bogoljubow
And Dr. Alekhine.

Joseph Alger

One Midsummer Morning

Thrushes will be singing
In the meadow still,
Timothy and clover
Ripening on the hill.
Nothing will be changed
Except the fact that we,
Being dead as doornails,
Shan't be there to see
Thrushes in the field nor
Hill where clover grows.
What we shall be doing
Heaven only knows.

Miriam Vedder

* Thus play, with strict punctilio
And Franco-Deutsch routine,
This Russian-born Bogoljubow,
This Slavic Alekhine.

172

A Tired Ballad of Travel

[BROUGHT ON BY AN EXHAUSTIVE PERUSAL OF THE ADVERTISEMENTS]

Say, do the balmy breezes blow on old Nantucket still?
Do flowery trails wind fragrantly along Sagachet Hill?
Are the rosy salmon leaping now in gray Columbia's waters?
And how is the Real Home Atmosphere at the Inn of the Seven
  Daughters?

>   In Yellowstone, in Yellowstone,
>   The foaming geysers play.
>   And likewise do
>   The fish that strew
>   The Road to Mandalay.
>   And trains and ships to take me there
>   Unendingly go by;
>   And I should seek like other folk
>   The plunging keel, the pouring smoke,
>   And the cinder in the eye.

Tell me how on Hawaiian shores the blue Pacific smiles.
And the glass-bottomed boats, do they still put out from the
  Catalina Isles?
And down by the wash of the tropic seas, where the cruising
  steamers stray,
Is the Air-Cooled Dining-Room worth the trip at eight-eighty-
  eight per day?

>   Switzerland's for plutocrats,
>   The brave deserve the Fair,
>   Ni-a-ga-ra
>   Is said to draw
>   The honeymooning pair.
>   The Whitneys go to Bailey's Beach

173

To bathe in waters saline,
And I should up at break of dawn
To take a trip at least upon
    The Hudson River Day Line!

I know that, tall, in Alaska now, the totems wait for me,
And little villages win the heart in Glorious Normandy;
That islanders pluck their gay guitars in Majorca, after dark,
And a very nice bus would carry me up, I think, to Asbury Park.

Vacation Time has come again.
    A Thousand Playgrounds call me!
And I would heed
Did not the need
    For action so appal me.
The flush is on the eastern sky,
    The liner's in the slip;
But the haze is also on the eye
    And the yawn upon the lip.
I'd board a train, I'd breast a wave,
    I'd mount an Alpine boulder.
But strenuous delights are those.
Ah, draw the shades and let me doze
    Above a travel folder.
                              Phyllis McGinley

Autobiography

"Everything's a vicious circle"—
I have worn that saying thin;
Now, I find, I'm much more vicious
Than the circles that I'm in.
                              Charmé Seeds

Reprise

Once it was hardly worth remark
When summer came to Central Park.
We looked across its well-trimmed sward
With a superior disregard,
Longing for woodlands undefiled
By traffic, shady nooks more wild,
While the Casino made poor Pan
Flee farther from the haunts of man.
How sad, we thought, these leafy dells
Full of the City's chaff and smells;
These lordly maples fouled by soot,
And Sunday papers underfoot!
Most condescendingly we'd take
Our evening turn around the lake,
Musing on Adirondack airs,
Campfires in Maine, or steamer chairs.
But you are there and I am here,
Which makes a difference, my dear!
I don't know what I'd give tonight
If we could share that simple rite
Of meeting somewhere after dark
And Driving Slowly Through the Park!
Say, are the swan boats out the same
As then, the squirrels just as tame?
And is the carrousel off key
Exactly as it used to be?
Those funny statues of The Great—
Do they still find us out of date?
It's not the heat of mid-July,
Or thunder blacking out the sky,
That I remember most of all,
But things like music on the Mall,
Lights twinkling in a myriad towers,
And one small window, which was ours!

Leslie Nelson Jennings

175

Moment in Marmalade

Hating to finish breakfast
as I do,
delaying time
in pantomime,
holding the watch-hand,
pouring coffee, and
reading the murder market on page two,
I say:
World, stay!
There's one thing still,
one moment shielding me
from what you want,
do what you will:
This bit of marmalade
which I've not ate,
this almost square of toast,
they'll save me yet.
Until I spread the one
upon the other,
brother,
until I shade
the edges carefully with my butter blade,
I am as safe as Ptolemy from time,
and I can hold
untold,
suspended in a spoon,
a thousand things sublime,
not offices or trade.
So I shall keep
the last bite to the last,
tasting in my mouth
the amber of the sun,
or deep
the qualmless South,

as one
saying goodbye, all's past,
goodbye once more,
and out the door.

David McCord

River Night

Up and down the river
The barges go:
Whether moons are yellow,
Whether stars flow
Softly over city,
Softly over town,
Sleepily the barges
Go up and down.

Up and down the river
On summer nights
The barges drift,
And emerald lights
And crimson prick
The darkness under
Blown-out stars
And gathering thunder.

Up and down the river
The barges go,
Up and down the darkness
River-winds blow,
And sleepers in a city
And sleepers in a town
Dream of the barges
Going up and down.

Frances Frost

177

Pavement Portraits

I. SUBWAY CHANGE MAN

He juggles the nickels,
  And jingles the dimes,
And duly dispenses the quarters;
He adds up his figures a great many times,
And furnishes sawdust for porters.

He's steward of transit,
  He's lord of the stiles,
He's underground usher-in-waiting;
He stacks up his wares in precarious piles,
And pushes them under his grating.

He counts every nickel
  That drops out of sight,
And eyes his machines with affection—
And just when the rush-hour has swarmed to its height,
With manner serene, and deliberate quite,
Emerges to make his collection.

II. MOTORMAN

He peers from his palpitant window,
Persuasively banging his bell,
And trekking a trail through the tangle
In the shade of the chequerboard "L."

And transit may roar and may rumble,
And traffic may ebb and may flow—
The motorman moves on his mission,
Serene and insistent and slow.

The taxis go swooping around him,
The truckmen cut under his nose—

He's cluttered with crowds at the crossings;
It's really a wonder he goes.

He doesn't pretend to be speedy,
He doesn't do tricks with a wheel;
He simply rides uptown and downtown
On a stately and uniform keel.

Burke Boyce

Flower Wagon

With potted blooms, and sprightly sprays
  And faint nostalgic powers,
It brings, among the city's ways,
  Its migratory bowers.

It paints a gay similitude
  Of something rather higher—
And seeks, with gentle pulchritude,
  The promise of a buyer.

Its rolling hubs, and ambling gait,
  And blossoms brightly vernal,
Proclaim the perfect delegate
  Of hope that springs eternal. . . .

Burke Boyce

Poem of Pain and Passion

Now we must abjure embraces,
Creep away, hide our faces,
Better far that we should part so
Till this sunburn doesn't smart so.

Leslie Pearl

"Pray, How Did You Manage to Do It?"

[AFTER SOUTHEY, CARROLL, AND 1929-1932]

"You are broke, Father William," the country cried;
  "The few stocks which are left you are low;
And yet you were constantly on the inside
  Just three little summers ago."

"In my youth," said Pa Bill, "I detested the crooks,
  Yet I wished to be very pecuniar;
So I modeled my life on the boys in the books
  Of Horatio Alger, Jr."

"You are broke, Father William," the country clucked,
  "And yet you have houses and land.
Why, I can remember the parties you chucked
  That must have cost twenty-five grand."

"In my youth," Pa declared, "I am bound to confess
  That I played like an elegant sport;
I believed in the bullish American press
  And I never sold anything short."

"You are flat, Father William," continued the kid,
  "And yet you own Central and Steel;
Your income from them must be not inconsid,
  And enough to buy many a meal."

"In my youth," Father William responded in part,
  "I took only expert advice;
And the wise ones who sold me the stocks on the mart
  Said: 'Never consider the price!'"

"You're in debt," said the country, "from spring until fall,
  And yet you have thousands of shares."

"I don't," said Pa Bill, "understand it at all";
And he kicked the whole country downstairs.

Franklin P. Adams

East Hampton

". . . and the sea always sounds better after the third."

Thalassa, Thalassa,
  Oinopa ponton:
the sea mad and turquoise,
the sea sapphire and friendly,
                    the gray unquiet sea;
the sea beating behind the vermouth cocktails,
the sea beating behind the sunburned females—
  O Eëlios! O Eëlios!
("Put on the eyebrow paint, sister;
Remember those brown legs, sister.")
                    —the gray unquiet sea
where Venus' white, white nakedness was first unfurled;
  whose roar once seemed to me
like all the winds in all the branches of the world.

Eleanor Davenport

Midsummer Melancholy

Oh, somewhere there are people who
Have nothing in the world to do
But sit upon the Pyrenees
And use the very special breeze
Provided for the people who
Have nothing in the world to do
But sit upon the Pyrenees
And use the . . .

Margaret Fishback

New England Meeting House

I can remember, as a little child,
The deep, warm wonder of the Sunday prayer.
Eyes shut fast—I knew—heart beating wild,
If I dared look, an angel would be there.

I knew the light changed, while my eyes were so,
I knew the church flew open to the air
And a pale-blue flame flickered to and fro
Just above the pulpit, to show the Word was there.

Yesterday I sat in church, eyes open wide,
And watched a tired man repeat the same remembered prayer—
There wasn't any angel standing at his side,
And just above the pulpit—no blue flame there.

Harold Trowbridge Pulsifer

The Lonely

There is no cold and crying place
That's crucified upon the pole
But has more sight of God's own face
Than any living soul.

There is no mountain, scarred and riven,
Whose height not even the beasts may span
But has more comradeship with Heaven
Than any living man.

And the strange and stony wilderness,
Whence all but day and night depart,
May drain a deeper loneliness
Out of the human heart.

Samuel Hoffenstein

Islander

Out of a universe of things
  These twain are for my stay:
Ocean, that walls me in;
  Time, that bears you away.

Muna Lee

Random Reflections

BIOLOGICAL

A girl whose cheeks are covered with paint
Has an advantage with me over one whose ain't.

INTROSPECTIVE

I would live all my life in nonchalance and insouciance
Were it not for making a living, which is rather a nouciance.

ARCHITECTURAL

I'd feel much better about the Grand Central Bldg.
If only the architect had left off the gldg.

LITERARY

Philo Vance
Needs a kick in the pance.

ON ICE-BREAKING

Candy
Is dandy
But liquor
Is quicker.

REMINISCENT

When I consider how my life is spent,
I hardly ever repent.

FUNEBRIAL

Among the anthropophagi
People's friends are people's sarcophagi.

THEATRICAL

In the "Vanities"
No one wears panities.

MONSTROUS

You take babies,
I'll take rabies.

Ogden Nash

5 P. M. Sunday

It is the weekend party's dreadful hour;
And tranquil davenport and padded chair
Cushion uneasy heads with tender care.
A tremulous matron dumbly prays for power
To last till bedtime. Jokers' voices ring
The changes on the theme of Friday night
And what we did when we were all so tight.
The host suggests a highball, shuddering.
The hostess smiles with holy self-control,
Even though broken glass and china cut
Her heart to ribbons, and a smoldering butt
Has burnt through dainty fabrics to her soul.
   She has to run to smother the pernicious
   Maid, who is singing as she does the dishes.

Morris Bishop

184

VIII. AUGUST: *Dozes the town*

Hymn to the Sun and Myself

Well! Well!
The day's at the morn!
Dandy old day!
Dandy old morn!
Oh! Look!
The hillside's dew-pearled!
Nicely old hillside!
Nicely dew-pearled!
And oh! Look!
The snail's on the thorn!
Lucky old snail!
Lucky old thorn!
Well! Well!
All's right with the world!
Hurrah for the right!
Hurrah for the world!

For oh! what a day it is today, my lads!
Oh! my lads, what a day it is today!
At 11:07 A.M. I'll be 27¾ years old,
An age dear to me because it was once passed through by Edna
  St. Vincent Millay.
Oh what fun to be young and healthy and alive
And privileged to do some of the work of the world from nine
  to five!
Oh let me be truly thankful for every one of those 27¾ years;
For not having been run over by the Lexington Avenue Express
  or gored by runaway steers;
For not having been able to afford a passage on the *Titanic,*
And for not having had any money to lose in the recent stock-
  market panic;
For never having written a best-seller, only to be wounded by
  the critics;

For never having gotten impeached for making millions in dirty
   politics;
For never having made any enemies by getting ahead too
   speedily;
For not finding the world at my feet while still as young as
   Lindbergh or Gertrude Ederle;
For not having tried to impress my girl but being naturaler with
   her and naturaler,
So that now, instead of having to marry and all that, I can be a
   jolly jilted baturaler;
Above all let me be thankful for something rarer than gold—
Viz: that at 11:07 A.M. I'll be 27¾ years old.
Oh let my future be as lucky as my past!
Oh let every day for a long time not be my last!

Ogden Nash

City Evening

The light that burned me up by day
Decides a little while to stay,
And writes a long and golden scrawl
In tree-leaf shadows on my wall.
The bulbous sun has spilled his fire,
Impaled upon a Jersey spire;
And hard day-objects of the street
Grow soft, in the long light, and sweet.
Noon's hot fortissimo still clings,
Muted in many murmurings;
And with the lingering light o'erspread
My thoughts are all new garmented.
Far down the block in yellow ease
Behind a row of gold-tipped trees
The "L," like some old dream, goes by
Betwixt the Avenue and sky.

E. B. White

Argument

Two stubborn beaks
Of equal strength
Can stretch a worm
To any length.
                Mildred Weston

Biarritz

But it was neither St. Cloud nor the Tuileries that made the Empress
happiest; it was Biarritz.—*Biography of the Empress Eugénie.*

Wind in the mimosas and a wind off the seas,
And a high wind blowing from the high Pyrenees:
Yonder lies Chiberta, yonder is Bayonne,
But who shall find the country where an Empress is gone?

All along the Côte des Basques rolls the silver spray;
Brown men and women pass in peignoir and béret;
But go and search the beaches and who that searches there
Shall catch a flash of eagles in the blue burning air?

Bathers from the Bellevue and the lofty Miramar
—Swim gaily, *messieurs-'dames,* but don't swim far!—
Loiter in the sunshine while the bright yachts cruise
And girls cry macaroons of Saint-Jean-de-Luz;

Girls cry carnations that are spicy out of Spain,
Girls cry *L'Intransigeants* that caught the Paris train,
But never at the noontide or in the twilight's peace
Does anybody cry now *"Vive l'Impératrice!"*

Up and down the roadways the swift Hispanos run,
Glittering with the laughter of the children of the sun;

And memory is a heavy thing for anyone to ask,
Trooping off for cocktails at the gay Bar Basque.

Lanvin and Molyneux, Jean Patou and Worth,
Their shops line the little streets like princes of the earth,
But never does an Empress descend at any house
For manteau or crinoline or Garibaldi blouse.

Never does an Emperor at any *gala* now
Tug at his imperial and make a courtly bow,
And who that go in *espadrilles* and *maillots* have a glance
For the ghostly promenadings of an Empress of France?

With her villa and her violets, her Pèpa and her son,
And her light airs from Offenbach that soothe and settle one,
With her black-lacquered carriage and her black-lacquered span
Clop-clopping down the road, driving toward Sedan!

Kenneth Allan Robinson

Sonnet

Sonnets are popular because they fill
   The empty spaces in a magazine.
Compact and frictionless as any pill,
   They can be swallowed almost without spleen.
No editor is ever criticized
   For printing sonnets. Everybody knows
That centuries ago they were devised
   By precepts it were foolish to oppose.
Poets adore the form that can exalt
   Their thinnest, hollowest, most bland conceit
Into the highly polished verbal vault
   Of fourteen lines and calm iambic feet.
As for the couplet—Shakespeare can be proud
   Of sewing them in such a perfect shroud!

Marya Mannes

Old Men and Young Men

Old men are full of zest and information,
And they remember all they ever thought.
Old men are vigorous in conversation.
Young men exist to listen and be taught.

Old men give dates that may not be disputed,
And they recall the parts old actors played.
A young man's fact is easily refuted:
He was not present when the world was made.

Old men are heartily opinionated.
Whatever young men do, the old have done,
In better ways that have not deviated.
The legend lies, that old men sit in the sun.
Old men, in great ambition unabated,
Stand proudly on their heads at eighty-one.

Young men are thin and shy, which is no wonder:
Young men need rest, and life allows them none.
The old men storm at them for every blunder:
Nothing is right young men have ever done.

Young men who tell a story twitch and stutter.
Their ears are large and red. Their hands are cold.
They speak too loud, or in despair they mutter,
And feel discouraged when the story's told.

Old men resent solicitude and hearses.
All they abstained from doing they regret.
Old men betrayed into the hands of nurses
Despise the scientific care they get,
And vow disgracefully, with terrible curses,
That they'll outlive the meddling woman yet.

John Holmes

Memo for an Unclaimed Pad

No. HP618389C

THE PHOENIX MUTUAL LIFE INSURANCE COMPANY
is reserving a genuine two-tone lambskin desk or pocket memorandum
pad, "Things to do Today," for E. B. White, whose name will be
embossed upon it in gold. It will be forwarded at once upon receipt
of this card at the Home Office.

While years, like clocks, run slowly down,
    And love lies curled in locket,
This patient pad in Hartford town
    Awaits my desk or pocket.

This lovely, lambskin, two-tone pad,
    Whose pages are construable,
Promising what the Phoenix had,
    To make my dust renewable.

This pad that shows at last a plan
    By which, when I retire,
I'll have what Phoenix says I can
    And thinks that I desire:

Money with which to do the things
    And get the things I want,
And safety that this money brings
    For son and wife and aunt.

Ah, lovely pad! Ah, lambskin pad!
    Fashioned of genuine leather!
The only things I want I've had:
    True love, and change of weather,

And one conviction, strong since birth,
    Which still I find incurable:

That none was ever born to earth
  Whose life was quite insurable.

No pad called "Things to do Today,"
  Though two-toned and refillable,
Could make me anything but fey,
  Or render me unkillable,

And though cold comfort for mine heirs,
  Yet comfort let it be,
That never were a day's affairs
  Predictable for me.

And let who finds the comfort cold
  Be never made less sad
To find my name embossed in gold
  Upon a lambskin pad.

E. B. White

Little Words

When you are strayed, there is nor bloom nor leaf
  Nor singing sea at night, nor silver birds.
And I may only stare, and shape my grief
  In little words.

I cannot conjure loveliness, to drown
  The bitter woe that racks my chords apart.
The staggering pen that sets my sorrow down
  Feeds at my heart.

There is no mercy in the shifting year;
  No beauty wraps me tenderly about.
I turn to little words—so you, my dear,
  Can spell them out.

Dorothy Parker

Answers to Famous Questions

I

Tell me, where is fancy bred,
Or in the heart, or in the head?
How begot, how nourished?
"The Merchant of Venice"

Fancy, boy, the kind you mean,
Comes directly from the bean.
Nine times out of ten it springs
From *her* like for lovely things.
Often *he,* no Mahatma Gandhi,
Wants his food and liquor handy.
We owe many masterpieces
To Altman's bill and three-year leases.

II

Oh, why should the spirit of mortal be proud?
William Knox

I know seven reasons, at least, why it should—
Any one plausible, all of them good;
But in view of the headlines we swallow each week,
It strikes me the spirit of mortal is meek.

III

Shall a woman's virtues move
Me to perish for her love?
George Wither

I shouldn't think so. History shows
The girls who rocked or ruined nations
Were, without one exception, those
With questionable reputations.

Baird Leonard

194

Saraband

M. Papanastasiou, agrarian candidate, has announced his intention of not contesting a seat in the Arcadian district.—*News Item from Greece.*

Hog-Face! Flap-Ear!
Here!
Snouty and Rump and Flick,
Quick!
Gallop and chatter,
Every satyr,
Snicker and wheeze
As you plunge through the trees—
Hahay! Hist!
This way, where the forest noon swims in a quivering mist,
By the rocks
Where the fountain's cool irony flatters and mocks
The birds, the sky,
And the laugh and the shriek of the girls as they scatter and fly—
Hai! Hai!
Cheeks aflame, legs wine-splashed, long strangled cry—
Hai! Yai!
As we run like the wind and leap hard on the prey—
Ohé!
Not today.
Hairy ones, cock your ears, listen now, for I say
Not today.
Not now.
Wow!
Let 'em fly, let 'em go,
Hairy ones, stand your ground in a grimacing row,
Pipe your eyes,
Clash hoofs, bite the earth, shake the trees with your stampings
  and sighs,
Hou! Hou!
Papanastasiou
Comes no more, comes no more, comes no more . . .

195

Hairy ones, bellow and roar,
Oi! Oi!
Otototoi . . . oi!
Hairy ones, what a boy!
Remember his Hat? Remember his Boots?
And the tempest of hoots
As we sped him each day on his way to the neighboring town
(Bob down!),
While the dark forest rang with our yells and our jeers
(Twig his ears!),
And the dolphins from here to Propontis leaped sniggering out
of the blue?
Hou!
Fled, fled is our joy,
(Otototoi . . . oi!)
Nevermore
Shall the sea-blue bird of the spring and the wave crashing green
on the desolate Thracian shore
Hear that scream
Like a cry in a dream
And tremble and waver and flee in terror afar—
(Har! Har!)
Hou!
Papanastasiou
Comes no more, comes no more . . .
Sore
Is our harsh hairy grief as we posture and prance,
Pirouette and advance,
And grinning retreat, as our shadows perform a grotesque
Arabesque
And we twirl and leap thrice, hoof to hoof, hand in hand,
In our sad saraband:
'Tototoi! Nevermore shall the—*Hark!*
Who goes there in the dark?
Who treads soft, snapping twigs?
Oh, figs!

196

A shadow. A bird. A gust in the trees . . .
Cocytus! What gray hairy terror swoops down on the breeze?
Look! Look! *Sauve qui peut!* On the left! On the lfffffffft!
Whrrrrrrrrrft!
Prrrrft!

(The forest is silent.)

D. B. Wyndham Lewis

The Pool

She stood as slim, as clear, as cool
As any birch beside this pool—
Then with a sudden curving dive
Made the dark water spring alive
With million ripples and the white
Flash of her body's free delight
As out across the reed-fringed bay
She plunged in wriggling naked play.

I would rather be the eyes that look
On her in this secluded nook
Than see all fabled queens afar—
The one who made the Trojan war,
The one who wrought the doom of kings,
The one who broke the minstrel's strings,
The one belovèd of the Swan,
Or any of all the beauties gone.

Dripping with drops that chase and glide,
Once more above the waterside
She poises with a little smile,
Natural, as if free from guile.
But well, supremely well, she knows
That she is colored like a rose,
And that my eyes are not yet dull,
And that a rose is beautiful.

Arthur Davison Ficke

Late August

Now like an unkempt wife, a blowsy napper,
  Yawning away the middle afternoon
In paper curlers and a cotton wrapper,
  Reluctant to bestir herself too soon,
Dozes the town. Boredom and heat assail her.
  These are the dusty, unimportant days
When bathing suits are cheap at Lord & Taylor,
And blondes go by in velveteen bérets.

Now fades the glamour of the sidewalk table.
  Penthouse and roof their early glitter lose,
And now the very weather is not able
  Longer to strut in masquerade as news.
Fails, even now, across the somnolent city,
The voice of Macy chiding his committee.

Phyllis McGinley

Poem of Praise ✓

Swift things are beautiful:
Swallows and deer,
And lightning that falls
Bright-veined and clear,
Rivers and meteors,
Wind in the wheat,
The strong-withered horse,
The runner's sure feet.

And slow things are beautiful:
The closing of day,
The pause of the wave
That curves downward to spray,
The ember that crumbles,

The opening flower,
And the ox that moves on
In the quiet of power.

Elizabeth Coatsworth

Summer Friendship

Yes, we were friends in those exciting days.
We sat discussing books on green park-seats,
Or drank the nights away in dim cafés,
Or sang at dawn along the empty streets.
He had an air of gaiety about him
That made all else seem trivial and small.
I used to wonder how I'd lived without him
So many years; I used to half recall
The odd ways I had sought for happiness
Before he'd made it such a simple thing.
He made all wealth seem foolish to possess,
He made an ancient myth of suffering.
Yes, we were friends, I'll say, because I must,
But one incredible day I seemed to wake
As from a lotus-dream, and all was dust
That we'd created for each other's sake.
I knew not what I lacked, nor learned of it,
But suddenly I stood appalled before
A mind not firm but hollowed out by wit,
A heart resembling some indifferent shore
Whereon the treasures of all wrecks were cast
And swept away as casually again.
And saddened by discovery at last,
I made an end of friendship, there and then.
Now he is gone with everything that passes,
Gone with the wind, gone with the April flowers.
We used to sing and click our brimming glasses,
And laugh and cheer the speeding of the hours.

Helene Mullins

Manhattan Epitaphs:
The Boss

The Boss
can no longer
give orders
here
and the clerks
bring garlands
and a crocodile
tear.

Alfred Kreymborg

Policy

A suit of sheep's clothing
I bought at the store;
To give to the wolf
Who lives at my door.

Carolyn Wells

Midsummer Night's Dream

Embodied souls
In pairs,
In honeyed twos
Frequent the parks,
Essay the avenues,
Wondering what deity
Could be invoked
That they'd be joined together,
Yet not yoked.

Mildred Weston

200

An Alley Cat

Mangy and gaunt I walk the tiles tonight,
And mangy comes my lady to her tryst;
And nine lives back (nine hundred some have guessed)
With prouder mien we rambled, ranging light.
Sacred and sleek, on roofs of amethyst
And eaves of ivory we wandered, while
A lotus-colored moon swung up the Nile,
And Memphis slumbered in a silver mist.

O it was heaven just to sit and be
Antiphonal beneath some royal room
Until, for all our sacredness, we heard
Loud hieroglyphic curses flowing free,
And marked a sandal hurtling through the gloom
Hot from the hand of Rameses the Third!

Nancy Byrd Turner

Atavian

And I, a woman of the twentieth century, am well aware
That all my love for you is an anachronism,
Something Byronic, Tennysonian, with even a dash of Felicia
    Hemans,
And something of "Friendship's Garland" and something of
    the Napoleonic wars.
  It is an anachronism, my love for you; it might be worked
    into mournful willowwreaths of hair, or expressed by a
    sonnet sequence in feminine rhymes and couplet ending:
  It might mold its desires chastely into a garland of waxen fruit,
    perfect in form and color, lifeless, ornamental, useless;
  It might be built into a pseudo-Gothic castle, turrets and ghost
    and drawbridge all complete;
  It might be Elizabethan-Arcadian or Victorian-Olympian; any
    sad, foolish, extravagant thing

Of an age that took its sentimental folly seriously.
But you, a product of this century,
Your mind a by-product of its mad towns, of New York and
    Madrid, London and Paris,
What, in the name of the four cities, could you ever do with
    my love?
And why cannot I follow the mode of my great-grandmother
    closer still
And lay the silly thing away
With a silly tear in its folds,
And in the riband neatly clasping it,
One little, pompous, declarative immortelle?

Muna Lee

Ghost of an Opera House

[DEDICATED TO ROBERT EDMOND JONES AND THE PRODUCTION OF
"THE MERRY WIDOW" IN CENTRAL CITY, COLORADO]

Gone are dim gas in crystal chandelier,
Flamboyant frescoes, flickering footlight-jets,
Weber and Verdi, solos and duets,
Blue smoke, and breaths of whiskey and of beer,
The curtain's gaily-colored gondolier,
The garish grandeur of the various sets!
Now, in the empty street, a white moon whets
The edge of night, and sparkling stars appear.

There lies the gulch where Matt McMan struck gold,
And sluiced his claim, and gathered in his dust—
Whence sprang the hillside-mines and streets of hell,
Masonic Hall and Opera House of old,
And that vast Franklin stove, since fallen to rust,
That jeweled the lobby of the Elite Hotel!

William Rose Benét

Girl in a Tree

Her legs were long
And scratched with thistle.
She had a deft,
Enchanting whistle.

Her hands were slim
But strong for lifting
Herself to trees
When winds were shifting,

And there she'd sit
And watch the birds,
And nibble twigs,
And juggle words;

And there she'd lean
And whistle clearly
Till she was God—
Or very nearly.

Frances Frost

Return

How can a woman tell
What she has seen
Who in the Realms of Love
Lately has been?

A broken sentence here,
A spread of hands,
Eyes that have seen the sun
In other lands—

So the explorers once
Back from New Spain
In draughty palace rooms
Tried to explain,

Tried to explain, explain,
Then, in despair,
Displayed an Indian
With feathered hair.

Elizabeth Coatsworth

Portrait

Caroline Million
Is a hundred years old:
She feels pretty good,
But her feet are awful cold.
She's sitting by the chimney
In a nice warm nook,
Fingering her false teeth
And the Lord's Good Book.
She's blinking in the firelight,
Blinking at the fire,
Blinking at her daughter,
Hot with desire
To kill her lumpy daughter
And feed her to the crows,
(Crows love fat meat
Everybody knows.)
Caroline Million
Is a hundred years old,
She feels pretty good,
But her feet are awful cold.

Isabel McLennan McMeekin

Songs of a Markedly Personal Nature

This is what I vow:
He shall have my heart to keep.
Sweetly will we stir and sleep
   All the years, as now.
Swift the measured sands may run;
Love like this is never done.
He and I are welded one—
   This is what I vow.

This is what I pray:
Keep him by me, tenderly;
Keep him sweet in pride of me
   Ever and a day.
Keep me from the old distress;
Let me, for our happiness,
Be the one to love the less—
   This is what I pray.

This is what I know:
Lovers' oaths are thin as rain.
Love's a prelude to a pain—
   Would it were not so!
Ever is my heart athirst,
Ever is my love accurst;
He is neither last nor first—
   This is what I know.

PROPHETIC HEART

Because your eyes are slant and slow,
   Because your hair is sweet to touch,
My heart is high again; but, oh,
   I doubt if this will get me much.

DE PROFUNDIS

Oh, is it, then, Utopian
To hope that I may meet a man
Who'll not relate, in accents suave,
The tales of girls he used to have?

INDIAN SUMMER

In youth, it was a way I had
    To do my best to please,
And change, with every passing lad,
    To suit his theories.

But now I know the things I know,
    And do the things I do;
And if you do not like me so,
    To hell, my love, with you!

Dorothy Parker

ix. SEPTEMBER: *A scarlet leaf*

Lost—Eighteen Per Cent

Newspapers report that the population of Manhattan has declined
eighteen per cent in the past year.

O lost Eighteen Per Cent,
Why were you not content?
Was it the rent?
The soot? The noise?
Was it the curse of small bad boys
Playing street tag, hell-bent
To skin a shin or crack a brain?
Was it the subways? Was it the rain
Splashed by a five-and-fifteen taxi
That jarred upon your ataraxy?

Was it the stench of gasoline?
Or maybe some faithless slot machine
That took your penny and gave you naught?
Or was it the thought
Of your getting caught
Forever in this racking grind,
With the better days of your life behind—
What with pay so small,
And a lease to be signed,
And the children growing up, and all?

O wise Eighteen Per Cent,
I wonder where you went:
To Radburn, where the houses grow
Model row on model row,
All set just so,
With safe and antiseptic streets
And baby carriages in fleets?
To Great Neck, where the actors sport,
And life is gay and tenures short?

To Bronxville, Rockaway, Mt. Kisco;
To Brighton Beach or San Francisco?
To Pelham for the social season,
Or Newark for no earthly reason?

I wonder if you're now content.
I wonder if you're glad you went.
Have you at last contrived to find
All the things you had in mind—
Escapement from this urban riot,
Peace, and certainty, and quiet,
A balanced greens-and-roughage diet?
Have you? I'm thinking I might try it.

John Ogden Whedon

Misery Loves Company

She washed her stockings
And brushed her hair
But never a breath
Of a bedtime prayer
Did she murmur.
She went to sleep instead
The minute she tucked
Herself in bed.

At eight in the morning
She dashed for the shower,
Dressed, and was off
In half an hour.
And she smacked her lips
For the thought did strike her
That there were millions
Exactly like her.

Margaret Fishback

People

Some people are popular with other people because their wit is
    pointed
And they can sing tenor and are double-jointed
And have had experiences in Papua and the New Hebrides
And have private anecdotes about public celebries,
And are bright and amusing in the entr'acte
And always do the right thing in backgammon and contr'acte.

Other people are unpopular with other people because they
    discuss Bertrand Russell
And keep wanting you to feel their muscle
And point out that your furniture is oak, not mahogany,
And tell you all about their ancestors and progeny
And advise you to move to a suburb
And get away from all this tumult and huburb.

Both kinds of people, however, will eventually succumb to
    acidity;
Or perhaps they will be victims of the humidity
Or even approach metempsychosis
Through the various stages of cirrhosis.
But whatever the manner of their passing may be
It's all all right with me.

Ogden Nash

Garlic and Roses

We have an exclusive Community Park
Where all of our offspring play until dark
With a nurse upon guard, and a mother or two,
Who smile at the children and watch what they do.
And so they are kept in this cosy retreat
From entering terrible Sullivan Street.

Oh, in Sullivan Street
Marinaro sells meat,
Agenzia Pascale
Is run by Ravalli,
And next to Pumpelli
The bland Jimmy Kelly
Mans a flourishing bar
And does it in par.

But back in exclusive Community Park,
Americans stroll and remark on Remarque
And Spengler and Trotzky and Hitler and Joyce,
De Kruif, Mussolini, and Senator Boice.
The boys in their knickers, the girls in their middies
All wholesomely play with the youngest of kiddies,
For the Phyllises, Arthurs, and Marys and Lotas
Have reflexes, norms, and intelligence quotas.

While out in the shambles of Sullivan Street,
Maria del Prado has sausage to eat;
Pietro is lighting a wonderful pyre—
The baby's old buggy is thrown on the fire.
Upsetting the ashcans, a nocturnal rite,
Is well executed by Guido tonight.
The sidewalks their bathroom, the pavement their park,
They sleep in the mornings and play after dark,
They relish their garlic and wieners and wine
And joyously pillage the motors in line,
For the Brunos, Francescas, and little Maries
Have inherited flaws and fixations and fleas.

And some day my daughter shall play, for a treat,
In gay, uninhibited Sullivan Street.

Lois Montross

Diligence and Sloth

When Diligence encounters Sloth
She feels acidulous and wroth.

Alas, these Simian extremes!
Our peevish toil, our vacant dreams.

Clarence Day

Cradle Piece

Above this colored island in the sky
The dusky stars and darker winds go by,
And night has cradled continents and seas
And the youngest fox beneath the mountain trees.
Inland upon this island for your head
The earth has fashioned grasses and a bed
Of emerald fern to close about your heart
Wherefrom the fingers of the day depart.

The dark is swinging and the dew is cold,
The dark is a cradle for a moon grown old;
Love is your beginning and your end,
Love is pain and beauty, never friend,
Love is ice that blackens the yellow south,
Love is silence on the singing mouth.

The night is swinging slowly and the stars
On the breast of chaos are the ancient scars
Of unremembered wars. O child, your head
Has found this planet an enduring bed:
Forget the coming years that are a stream
Of mountain water falling down a dream. . . .
Forget the rocking island and the deep
Foreknown unrest. . . . Cry once again and sleep.

Frances Frost

213

Lines to Dr. Ditmars

[BY ONE WHO OBSERVED HIM FILLING OUT HIS CUSTOMS DECLARATION IN THE LOUNGE OF THE S.S. "NERISSA," SEPTEMBER 6TH]

Here between lunch and tea time, and days and hours between
The wash from the Orinoco and the vast Sargasso green,
As I watch you sitting and brooding, fitfully biting your pen,
I wonder: Are you, too, tempted, even as other men?

Is it thoughts like these you are thinking, here on the ocean plain,
Far from the wave-washed Bocas, distant from Port of Spain,
When the last of the loveless Virgins has vanished into the sea:
"How many boa constrictors can I take in duty-free?

"Touching those fer-de-lances I found in that little place
—Why am I always chasing more than I meant to chase?—
Is it wrong to forget to declare them; would anyone count it
    amiss?
I could carry them in my pockets if only they wouldn't hiss!

"And my coral snakes, capital fellows"—your brow is creased in
    a frown—
"I fear I've exceeded my quota; do I *have* to put them down?
Why couldn't some of us *wear* them? Is anyone bound to know
That we didn't have them with us when we sailed three weeks
    ago?

"My vampire bats are no trouble"—your dark frown lightens and
    lifts—
"Touristy trifles, I'll grant you, but they *do* make excellent gifts.
And I hope that the chaps at Customs who rummage among my
    things
Will keep if they can from mussing my bushmaster's loops and
    rings."

214

The trade winds stir at the curtains; the dark is beginning to fall,
But your features are firm with purpose: "No, I'll declare them
all.
I never was good at deceiving, and what excuse could I make
If the man reached into my luggage and pulled out a nine-foot
snake?

"Conscience is always conscience; if there's some slight duty to
pay,
One doesn't come back from a journey with a bushmaster every
day."
So you write out your declaration, with a firm, deliberate pen,
Down to the last little lizard, even as other men.

Kenneth Allan Robinson

Thoughts on the Cavalier Poets

[AT THE CORNER OF FIFTY-SEVENTH AND LEXINGTON]

Lovelace never spent his teens
Upon a thoroughfare to Queens,
And, written to the sounds of blasting,
Suckling's lines might be less lasting.
Waller wasn't driven daft
By honking automotive craft,
Nor can I think that riveting
Inspired Crashaw's thoughts on spring.
The rumble of the subway train
Was never dinned in Herbert's brain;
And when he penned that charming note
To Julia's silken petticoat,
It's more than probable that Herrick
Wasn't gazing at a derrick.

Parke Cummings

Party Toward Midnight

Here in one small mellow room
are joy, suspicion, fear, and hate;
and lurking in the corner's gloom,
envy and love stand disparate.

And one may school his lips and smile,
and one may speak and one may sigh;
but through our postures all the while
Time marches, putting moments by;

strides on inexorably, apart
from passion, hope, and enmity,
bestowing on each separate heart
a brief and sweet mortality.

Frances Frost

Apples in New Hampshire

Long poles support the branches of the orchards in New
Hampshire,
Each bough fruited closely enough to take a prize;
The apple crop is heavy this year in New Hampshire:
Baldwins, McIntoshes, Winesaps, Northern Spies.
Hay is heaped in cocks on the sloping floors of the orchards,
So that none of the fruit may be lost in the tangled grasses.
Let the sun lie a few weeks more against the boughs of the
orchards;
It will not be long before September passes.
The dew stands thickly beaded on the reddening cheeks of apples
When the sluggard autumn sun breaks through the mists;
Even when the moon shines, in the hard green apples
Ivory seeds blacken and ripening persists.

Sound core, wormy core, bruised and bitten,
The farmers' men will harvest them, heap after heap;
They will pick the best for market, they will shake the boughs
  and gather
Apples for cider, apples to keep.
Dark and cold in the earthy cellar,
Packed in barrels, laid upon shelves,
Filling the darkness with the redolence of summer,
Waiting for the children to help themselves,
White teeth piercing the glossy skins of apples—
The juice spurts and the cores are sweet and mellow;
There will be enough to last until March,
When the red skins wither and the pulp turns yellow.

And the bleak trees dreaming in the sharp still moonlight,
Snow nested in the crotches, rotted windfalls on the ground,
Will remember apples vaguely like a flood long remembered,
A mighty weight of apples, greedy and round,
Dragging their straining boughs lower and lower,
Sapping roots of their slow honey, stealing the dew.
The apple crop is heavy this year in New Hampshire;
Next year the trees will rest and apples will be few.

                                       Marie Gilchrist

Manhattan Epitaphs: Schoolmarm

One last
dumb
little lad
has come
who divides
or subtracts
what she asked him
to add.
          Alfred Kreymborg

Littoral

The bay-leaf juices give a scent
Of sun and sea to sea and sun.
Beneath slow wings by sea birds bent,
The shadows of the sea birds run.

The seethe of sweet salt at the weed
Spills upon mollusc and on snail.
Deep down the sharp-toothed tautogs feed
Rocked in a silty-colored gale.

The breast, the breathing of the sea
Feeds the marked shoreline's belted world,
Sea stars and strange lives fixed and free,
Anemones in bloom and furled.

The sun is warm upon the rocks.
Death's but a mouthful for a mouth
Here where no word of wisdom mocks
The light of north, west, east, or south.

The mollusc knows what house to raise
About his life. He builds that shell
Out of the water, not for praise,
For nothing but to serve him well.

And if the sea's breath, last indrawn,
Should cease, the mollusc, so betrayed,
Would wither on his kelpy lawn
Because in such wise earth was made.

And over all the earth's green chords
Would creep the black dry tints of hell,
Even to the level of men's words.
None would fare better than the shell.

Raymond Holden

218

Prelude

Assurance can come from nothing, or almost nothing;
the imperceptible accretion of trifles;
the delay in a gesture, the hesitation in a word,
the mistaken speech, acknowledged, or unacknowledged,
the penetration of a deception; it can come
from observation of what has been unobserved:
new knowledge of an old history, new sight
of a known face, a known field; the path
familiar to the foot, but with surprises,
a raw pebble, dislodged by rain, a scarlet leaf
drowned in a puddle, a branch of maple to brush the sleeve,
or such other casuals. It can come
with a change of weather, the sundrawn mist
exaggerating softly the shape of a tree, snow
altering the face of a house, so that you guess
but do not know, yet triumph in knowing. Or can come,
and this is best, from the renewed inspection
of a known thing, and long loved; something small,
something tiny, but loved. The pimpernel,
hidden, with dusty petals, in deep grass,
obscure but always remembered, clear and
delicate, but with something obtuse as well,
obtuse and infinitesimal—this is the sort
of well-loving, and well-knowing, that changes
Tuesday to Wednesday.
                    Why not, or why,
have Wednesday for Tuesday? This is a question
which neither the heart nor calendar can answer.
But if assurance can feed itself on change,
change, then, and be assured.

Conrad Aiken

Country Night

She lived in terror of the country night;
As soon as afternoon began to fade
She went about the house, lit every light,
Bolted the doors, and drew each windowshade.
The house was like a ship that slowly listed,
The night was water, and it seemed to her
It rose relentlessly and unresisted,
Inevitable, black, and sinister.
The little liquid noises that she heard
Were friendly and familiar things by day:
Tree and insect, flower and grass and bird,
Nothing at all to frighten her this way—
But still the night rose higher, till it found
Her tense and quivering and almost drowned.

Selma Robinson

To an Insect, Flying About in Church

Small Pilot of a most exclusive plane,
What dazzling hope of insectivian gain,
What shining goal, what gleam across the night,
Inspired you to attempt this solo flight?
How pitifully brave you were, to dare
This region of ecclesiastic air,
To steer thus valiantly above my pew
The little buzzing motor that is You!
Alas, my friend, you have not long to wait
A sad but quite inevitable fate,
Crashing at last, in terror and distress,
Somewhere amid this wooden wilderness!

Sara Henderson Hay

Mosaic

Who, in the conduct of official duty,
Covers our unkempt Empire State with beauty?
Who is it voters, mindful not of party,
Acclaim with plaudits merited and hearty?
Who, the depression unending
Notwithstanding,
Biblically doubles each grassy blade,
Renews the green, augments the shade,
Making our pathway truly one of roses?
Obviously, Bob Moses.

The unemployed get work
To aid in his pet work
Of weaving a network
Of new ways
And through ways.
Each village and county,
Including Oswego,
Schoharie, Otsego,
Is blessed with his bounty.

For mister and madam
He spreads the macadam,
He smooths and massages—
They fly past garages
And hamlets and churches
And hemlocks and birches,
And, as they alight to pour gas in their tanks,
And smear on the mustard and gobble the franks,
They pause to give thanks.

(Gather up the orange peels,
Gather up the eggshells,

Pick up all the papers
And stick 'em in the can!)

He cares for the lambs
And the ewes and the rams,
The gnus and the yaks and the camels,
And the higher assortment of mammals—
The Swedes and the Poles and the Cabots,
The Murphys, the Cohns, and the Babbitts.
Each creature of the jungle, O!
Enjoys its private bungalow,
An air-conditioned, Kitchenetted bungalow.

The cricket, bee, and humble ant
Combine in one delirious chant,
And, as the bright day closes,
The bird who in the waning light
Was wont to call "Bob White! Bob White!"
Now cries instead "Bob Moses!"

(Dancing on the Mall,
Jazz for one and all;
We'll trip the light fantastic
In the moonlight on the Mall!)

All dingy and dark ways
He turns into parkways;
The swampy and gray ground
Soon blossoms as playground;
The withering landscape he sprinkles
And coaxes to life till it twinkles.
He renders first aid with his tonics
To shrubs when they wilt in the Bronix.
He dredges the inlets
For froglets and finlets,
He opens the outlets

For travelling troutlets,
For Moses is king of the ooze—
He is—the magical king of the ooze.
He cleanses the dune and develops the beach
As far as his wide jurisdiction will reach,
And, finally, banishes squatters—
And yachters.

(Jones's Beach is broad and clean,
Broad and clean, broad and clean,
Jones's Beach is broad and clean,
My tan lady.)

He neither sleeps nor loafs nor dozes,
But digs and plants and sprays and hoses.
He leads us, with unfaltering hand,
Straight down into the Promised Land,
And is it grand? Boy, is it grand?
And is it hard to understand
Why anyone composes
A psalm in praise of Moses?

Melville Cane

Bohemia

Authors and actors and artists and such
Never know nothing, and never know much.
Sculptors and singers and those of their kidney
Tell their affairs from Seattle to Sydney.
Playwrights and poets and such horses' necks
Start off from anywhere, end up at sex.
Diarists, critics, and similar roe
Never say nothing, and never say no.
People Who Do Things exceed my endurance;
God, for a man who solicits insurance!

Dorothy Parker

Monday, Tuesday, Wednesday—

He wraps injustice round him like a cloak, in
Which he parades, preposterously lone.
Life's pastry lies about her, mashed and broken,
Wasting its custard on a paving stone.
In high steel frames men trick grim death on girders,
In dark deep mines men grope the damp like moles,
Side streets of cities teem with thefts and murders,
In marble libraries aspiring souls
Sleuth the Great Word. . . . Mr. and Mrs. X
Dramatize contrarieties of sex.

He lights a cigarette and slumps aloof.
She flirts her lipstick out and wetly sighs.
A furtive wind is prowling round their roof,
The city stares—an octopus of eyes—
Pouring its darkness forth like inky fluid. . . .
His hands are jittery on the radio.
The street moon, golden sickle of a druid,
Gleams, reaping here no silvery mistletoe
Worshipped with blood-rites. . . . Yet their curious plight,
On second thought, might welcome such a rite!

He tries a book. She tries a magazine.
Within them both deep indignation swells.
Around them their apartment glows serene
Among a thousand like upholstered hells.
Their paths to this *impasse* defy analysis,
Save that the trivial now is grown so huge
As to induce in both complete paralysis
Of reason and resort to subterfuge.
Their burning wrongs sing ringing in their brains,
The oldest and the dismalest refrains.

Was it the theatre tickets or a gown
Or either's lateness or a chance remark?
High in the serried cliffs all over town,
Souls of a similar tinder wait the spark
That flares monotony with sudden color,
Jangling nerves jangled by the telephone,
And, after vivid eruption, renders duller
Than ever lives such as these two have known;
For now they pant with pain, these folk methodical,
Like people in their favorite periodical.

So doors will slam and voices shrill and bicker,
And she will weep and he will growl and curse,
Till fury is diminished to a flicker
As both decide they'd hardly feel much worse
If they were friends; and then in ways circuitous
One will apologize and one forgive.
Charges and plaints and grievances gratuitous
Will all be gently shaken in a sieve
Of moans and whimpers—till their rancor dies
In surfeit of emotional exercise.

A molten heat is raving at earth's core,
And deep through heaven rush planets clothed in flame,
The far-off jungles, the deep oceans roar,
The homeless tread a darkness without name,
The wretched groan in chains, the more defiant
Stride under baleful stars with starrier thirst,
Life shakes the mortal soul as might a giant
Rage against obdurate bars he fain would burst. . . .
But slumber's bumblings, in mellifluous key,
Now roam the bedroom of Apartment D!

William Rose Benét

Etiquette

Oh, where can one insult a man?
  The times are few, at most.
One can't insult a man at home,
  Because one is his host.

Oh, where can one insult a man?
  It's difficult, at best;
One can't insult him at his house,
  Because one is his guest.

Yes, where can one insult a man?
  It never is allowed.
One can't insult a man abroad,
  Because one draws a crowd.

I've wanted to insult a man;
  I've never done it yet.
It isn't magnanimity;
  It's merely etiquette.

Sylvia Fuller

Dispraising Tact

As a matter of fact
  Girls more sweet than clever
  Gain nothing whatever
By tact.

As well-beloved guests
  Their hostesses greet them,
  Proceeding to seat them
By pests.

The old ladies pet them
  And ask them to visit—
  Quite pleasant, but what does it
Get them?

And thrifty old codgers
   Prefer them as spouses
   To run gloomy houses
With lodgers.

Quite honestly, tact is
   A dangerous virtue
   And one it may hurt you
To practice!

Angela Cypher

A Congenital Lecturer Abroad

He talked of everything he'd seen,
He talked of everywhere he'd been,
He talked of paintings at the Pitti,
He talked of places in the City
Where one could drink till after two,
He talked of people that he knew,
He talked, with less than no inciting,
About the book that he was writing,
He talked at length about the heat,
He talked of what he liked to eat,
He offered several orations
Upon the history of nations.
He talked from breakfast until tea
Whenever he got hold of me,
Until I simply turned and ran
As soon as I beheld the man.
One day he drove up in a carriage
And talked officially of marriage.
He gave me time to tell him no,
Then, talking still, he rose to go.
Somewhere, wherever he has gone,
He's talking, talking, talking on.

Miriam Vedder

Rainy Night

Ghosts of all my lovely sins,
  Who attend too well my pillow,
Gay the wanton rain begins;
  Hide the limp and tearful willow,

Turn aside your eyes and ears,
  Trail away your robes of sorrow.
You shall have my further years—
  You shall walk with me tomorrow.

I am sister to the rain;
  Fey and sudden and unholy,
Petulant at the windowpane,
  Quickly lost, remembered slowly.

I have lived with shades, a shade;
  I am hung with graveyard flowers.
Let me be tonight arrayed
  In the silver of the showers.

Every fragile thing shall rust;
  When another April passes
I may be a furry dust,
  Sifting through the brittle grasses.

All sweet sins shall be forgot.
  Who will live to tell their siring?
Hear me now, nor let me rot
  Wistful still, and still aspiring.

Ghosts of dear temptations, heed;
  I am frail, be you forgiving.

See you not that I have need
  To be living with the living?

Sail, tonight, the Styx's breast;
  Glide among the dim processions
Of the exquisite unblest.
  Spirit of my shared transgressions.

Roam with young Persephone,
  Plucking poppies for your slumber . . .
With the morrow, there shall be
  One more wraith among your number.

Dorothy Parker

To a Cat

If Peace and Silence could arise
And walk, and look with living eyes,
And Night her starry cross descend
And stretch herself and be my friend
For shrimps and beef—I'm certain that
They'd be yourself, imperial cat!

You shame of all your jungle sires,
Of tiger-lords and panther-squires,
Well may these mighty warriors spare
To my distress your royal air—
I to my species, you to theirs
Apostate in adjoining chairs.

Here in this little room we dream
Amendments to the primal scheme:
You in your feline terms, of ease,
Catnip, and such urbanities;
I, of a jungle strength to dare to
Smite the three-score ills I'm heir to.

Samuel Hoffenstein

Epitaph for a Grim Woman

Sharp as sword of Saracen,
    Her fierce, New England pride:
She whetted it for years, and then
    She fell on it and died!

Patience Eden

Come, Sweet Culture, Prithee Come!

Walter Russell, president of the Society of Arts and Sciences, has announced a campaign, similar to the NRA drive, to raise the cultural standards of the American people.

Come, sweet culture, prithee come!
    Raise the standard of our living;
Let us join the mighty tussle
Led by President Walter Russell,
    Beauty now invade each home,
        Joy to all giving!

Light the ballroom of the Astor,
    Launch the nationwide offensive;
Let each active district leader
Tell his district's Muse we need her,
    Culture's drive grow ever faster,
        More intensive!

Deck the chart with colored pins
    To record the march of Beauty!
U. S. culture won't repay one
Till it's absolutely A-1;
    Foursquare genius always wins!
        Do your duty!

To the humblest home utensil
    Bring the benefit of streamline;

Grant the poets of our nation
Air-conditioned inspiration;
  Make the eversharpened pencil
    Toe the dreamline.

Come, sweet culture, prithee come,
  Art is long and life is fleeting;
Twine all gracious things and rare
In this crazy country's hair;
  Let no aesthete's harvest home
    Take a beating!

E. B. White

Dirty Looks

A grim and iron-visaged throng,
The motor-drivers roar along
Through fragrant fields and shady nooks
And give each other dirty looks.
Their fellow-man they blight with scorn
Because he did not blow his horn,
Because he blew too loud a blast,
Because he drove ahead too fast,
Because he lagged and blocked the way
And failed to spurt around that dray,
Because he passed upon a hill
Or on a curve; or, if you will,
Because derisively they marked
Some fault in how he backed and parked.
Howe'er that be, as on they go
In fruitless hurry to and fro,
With pregnant lips and baneful eyes
The motor-drivers stigmatize
Their fellow-men as fools and crooks
And give each other dirty looks.

Arthur Guiterman

A Connecticut Lad

[WITH A BAG OF POPCORN FOR A. E. HOUSMAN]

When first my way to fair I took,
  Danbury's hills were high,
And long I used to stand and look
  At trotting mares go by.

The elms were tall beside the turn
  And sulky wheels were red,
And few the pence that I'd to burn
  And light the heels that sped.

Now times are altered: hills are low,
  And when I take to fair
'Tis likelier lads than I who go
  To stand and watch a mare.

For now that I have pence in bank
  I pause with earnest face
Beside a concrete septic tank
  To drain a country place.

E. B. White

x. OCTOBER: *When the apple falls*

For Any Improbable She

What shall I do with So-and-So?
She won't say Yes and she won't say No.
She tiptoes around the cunningest traps
With a smile and murmur of Perhaps.
At nine I'm Darling, at ten I'm You—
Tell me, what is a man to do
When a lady his life is based upon
Likes to be wooed but won't be won?

What shall I do with So-and-So?
She won't say Come and she won't say Go.
I'm on my way, but I don't know where
I wouldn't care, if I didn't care.
Damn the man who invented the story
That a little suspense is salutory.
I swear by lipstick and powder puff,
Fun is fun, and enough's enough.

What shall I do with So-and-So?
She confesses that I am her favorite beau;
But let the topic of marriage arise
And see the astonishment in her eyes!
Why am I chosen so to be harried?
Other people have gotten married.
Is every courtship conducted thus
Or is it only confined to us?

What shall I do with So-and-So?
If it isn't Yes it must be No,
And a wise young man would never wait
Long enough to be given the gate.
On the other hand there's another guess—
If it isn't No it might be Yes.
Ah, she's got me and got me right.
Darling, what are you doing tonight?
                                        Ogden Nash

235

Caribbean Noon

The bellflower sky is hung
With a golden clapper tongue;
From the sea's dark lotus cup
Spark to gold spark gleams up.
All firmamental blue
Is molten in these two;
All terrestrial gold
These burnished stamens hold:
Vast sea petals that underlie
Vaster petals of widening sky.

Muna Lee

En Passant

The face the most fair to our vision allowed
Is the one we encounter and lose in the crowd.

Owen Meredith in "Lucille"

When I am driving home at night
    From wheresoever I have been,
And draw up, at the traffic light,
    Besides some lovely limousine,
I oftentimes exchange a glance
    With a delightful dame or squire
En route from dinner, drama, dance,
    In glad and glorious attire.

"How full the world is," I reflect,
    "Of people I shall never know,
Who might have an immense effect
    Upon the way my fortunes go!"
The chances are, the squire or dame
    Of pleasant anonymity
Is having pretty much the same
    Reaction in regard to me.

Of course one cannot sit and stare
  At perfect strangers in the street;
For citizens of *savoir faire*
  Such etiquette is indiscreet.
So, if the pause is long enough,
  With fine indifference I use
My lipstick or my powder-puff,
  And gaze at St. Bartholomew's.

Baird Leonard

Liz

Her mouth is a penny
Smudged with paint;
She isn't any
Like a saint.

Her eyes are beads
Of shiny black;
Her legs, slim steeds
That canter and clack.

She wears her thumbs
Inside her pockets;
She feasts on crumbs
And rides skyrockets.

Her conscience is tied
With scarlet bows;
She points with pride
To her button nose.

She clutters her days
With tinkling things;
Each night she prays
And feels for wings.

Her voice is a fiddle
Tuned more or less;
Her heart is a riddle
No priest may guess.
Dorothy Belle Flanagan

Hunters' Moon

On a gusty autumn evening,
O, the house was dull;
I slipped out adventuring
—And found the moon full!

The wind blew sharp and tangy
As I crossed the Square;
Little trees tossed shivering
Branches in the air.

Fourth was bright and bawdy,
Music in my ears,
Copper bangles, strings of beads,
Green as mermaids' tears.

Lower Sixth lay desolate,
Stark beneath the sky
As devastated Belgium, with
The moon riding high.

Minetta curved, a village street,
Crookedly and dark,
Distant voices singing
And a lone dog's bark.

Soup, at Romany Marie's,
Was cabbagey and hot,
And the yellow, flaunting moon
I think I forgot.

Frances Park

Harold Olney Pim

A man I love to contemplate is Harold Olney Pim,
So well turned out, so blandly stout, so placid, yet so trim!
His surface is perfection, his manners are refined—
And oh, the soft effulgence of his gentlemanly mind!

Through a world of care and crudity, of passion and of pain,
He glides on Super-Luxe Balloons, air-cushioned. All in vain
The Cyclone of Modernity that musses other men
Assails him—calm as Daniel in the well-known Lions' Den.

What secret has he hit upon, what esoteric lore
Preserves him from the conflict, the carnage, and the gore?
Is he a blameless Adept who keeps a Crystal Ball?
Is he a Christian Scientist? A Stoic? Not at all.

Dear Harold, in the first place, inherited a cool
Two millions; in the second place, he never went to school
Because his health was delicate, and also, it is true,
Because the gods withheld from him the requisite I.Q.

No, nothing worries Harold, for he is not inclined
To overtrain the muscles of an unathletic mind;
His bank account is ample, his soul is free from cramps,
And he speeds the hours collecting Chinese jade and postage
  stamps.

O happy Harold Olney Pim, if sad humanity
Could but learn the precious lesson that thou hast taught to me!
Utopian contentment would lap the earth, 'tis clear,
If God's chillun *all* were morons with a hundred thou a year!
                                        Lee Wilson Dodd

Hen-Party

The pack gathers
on the black Sunday.
Mrs. Lathers
and Mrs. Grundy
give a party
for all the bitches;
the food is hearty,
there are no hitches;
one stitches,
another chatters,
all blather
of small matters.

A-sudden enter
in agèd ermine,
the Queen-viper,
the Ace of vermin;
(the Pied Piper
overlooked her,
Cotton Mather
should have cooked her;)
a clacking racket,
a great stir,
in the center
the dowager.

Old Hecate
comes seldom,
each hag
and hell-beldam
tells the scandal,
bites a sandwich,

and burns a candle
to the Grand Witch.

After the curses
and incantations,
fetch the hearses
for the reputations!
                    Peggy Bacon

Night Walk

I heard one heavy apple fall
Down through the leaves, and that was all;

So still the air, that thudding sound
Was like a drumbeat on the ground.

There in the flat, unheated light
Of half a moon, I knew the night

Had offered me a secret token,
As if a single word were spoken

To show a ready apple must
Desert the branch to seek the dust.

A cow upon the pasture hill
Clanged at its bell, and then was still;

The other apples in the tree
Hung in a shadowed mystery;

I saw them darkly waiting there,
All in the hush of moonlit air.
                    Martha Banning Thomas

241

Marginal Notes

From Hollywood, Cal., to Boston, Mass.,
   Atlanta to the sea,
Culture is rearing its ugly pate,
And the word's gone forth you must cultivate
   Your personality.
By exercising on greens and horses,
By reading books and by taking courses,
By eating meals that are chiefly lamb,
By breathing straight from the diaphragm,
By counting ten when your temper rises
   And answering wrath in a gentle tone,
By startling people with odd surprises
   Like knowing French or the saxophone,
By banishing Error and slaying Fear,
By seeing your dentist twice a year,
You, too, may shine like the morning star,
Healthy, scintillant, popular,
Loved by those who are not your cousins,
Naming your friends by the scores and dozens,
Counting your friends by the throngs and bands,
Like the Junior League or the ocean sands.

Well, charm is a quality notable,
   That I probably can't claim any of.
But list to a lady who still contends,
Take it all in all, that a Host of Friends
   Is what you can have too many of.
For every comrade who's entertaining,
Rich in umbrellas when rain is raining,

Quick to kindle and slow to freeze,
You'll find eleven or so like these:
Friends suburban who jeer at cities
    And live for gardens and whitewashed pickets;
Serious friends who join committees
    And sign petitions and sell you tickets;
Friends confiding who Bare their Soul;
Friends who stand on their heads and roll;
Friends whose parties are simply riots;
Matchmaking friends and friends on diets;
Cynical friends who look askance
And say its featlier done in France;
Friends inquisitive, dull, or mocking;
Strenuous friends who take you walking;
Friends who worry about their looks;
Friends who borrow your favorite books;
Friends whose pity bedews you dankly;
Friends who feel they must tell you frankly;
Erudite friends who bow you down;
    Friends who dote on a national hookup;
Absent friends with a friend in town
    That, willy-nilly, you've got to look up;
Friends depressed by the Cosmic Riddle;
Musical friends who play the fiddle;
And just when the budget is almost treed,
Finally, certainly, friends in need.

MORAL

Relations are errors that Nature makes.
    Your spouse you can put on the shelf.
But your friends, dear friends, are the quaint mistakes
    You always commit yourself.

                                    Phyllis McGinley

A Sad Song About Greenwich Village

She lives in a garret
  Up a haunted stair,
And even when she's frightened
  There's nobody to care.

She cooks so small a dinner
  She dines on the smell,
And even if she's hungry
  There's nobody to tell.

She sweeps her musty lodging
  As the dawn steals near,
And even when she's crying
  There's nobody to hear.

I haven't seen my neighbor
  Since a long time ago,
And even if she's dead
  There's nobody to know.

Frances Park

A Good Reporter

Was Helen then so starry-eyed?
Was Troy so very tall?
And were the windy plains so wide?
Was there a Horse at all?

Perhaps they told old Homer
Things were of different size.
Perhaps a returning roamer
Told tales for blinded eyes.

But the blind man heard them, yearning,
So he raised his lyre and sang,
And the topless towers were burning,
And the plains with battle rang,

And Helen's face went launching ships,
The young died, and the hoary,
And Troy is down in dust and chips
—And Homer got the story.

Rollin Kirby

Song of the Open Road

I think that I shall never see
A billboard lovely as a tree.
Perhaps, unless the billboards fall,
I'll never see a tree at all.

Ogden Nash

Merely Hearsay

Some people do not go to bed
At night, but stay awake instead.
They feel the darkest hours to be
The choicest in eternity.
They think quite wonderful and deep
Thoughts when the world has gone to sleep.
At one or quarter past they can
Highly approve their fellow-man.
They grow articulate and do
Say very witty things at two.
At three their powers are at such height
They sing together, and recite.
This sometimes lasts till after four.

At five, when dawn is at the door,
A number of them still are able
To play at tag around a table.
At six, when daylight's really there,
They wash their faces, brush their hair,
And, with reluctance, go to bed.
Or so I've heard, and so I've read.

Miriam Vedder

Sermon in Staccato

Spurn me, leave me
If he will,
I can keep my
Head high still.

Only if he
Yields, shall he
Know my true
Humility.

Eleanor Chase

To a Taxi-Driver
Intent on Having the Island to Himself

Run me down and there will be
One less opportunity
For the likes of you to snare
This potential lady fare.

Toot and scramble as you go,
Make the common census show
One less customer at large
For your ostentatious barge.

Mow us down, relentless fool,
Mow us down in droves, and you'll
Find yourself alone at last
With your checkered taxi past.

Margaret Fishback

Crêpe

Grief begs sympathy with cold black silk,
Grief wants pity as a cat wants milk,
Grief for the living, grief for the dead,
Grief wants a hand and a shake of the head,
Grief is a gray cat
Sitting on the bed.
Grief is a stray cat,
Goes where she's fed.

Robert Hyde

Oversonnet

Smoke in the autumn, the cruel chemistry
Of leaf and wood set burning under big trees and beyond stone
  walls,
Smells suddenly of summer, of loam, and rain; all three
To seed and blossom, yield, and grow brown when the apple falls.
I put out my hand. This corner of gold was maple,
Coined by an angry frost, still smouldering as I touch;
The field is full of the lovely and the old, the garnered staple,
The leafy ruin raked in piles that burn too much.
Autumn came down in the night with the wind across the
  orchard,
Easily, far-forth, deliberate, brilliant with anvil flare:
Pouring the crucibled wealth of June out of the tortured
Leaves that quietly stir now and trample in the morning air.
I smell the blue smoke, I smell its sweet bitter grain,
Carrying foliage to the trees again.

David McCord

247

Divine Discontent

She has builded herself
A private hell
About the size
Of a walnut shell,
And curled herself
Tight up therein
With miserable knees
As high as her chin.
Cramped stiff,
She is doubtless happy,
But—
She begins to suspect
(I know;
I can tell)
She should have built
A roomier hell,
For a little company's
Just as well.

Florence S. Edsall

Malice Domestic

A Mrs. Shepherd of Danbury, Conn.,
She tried to steal our cook,
She may have thought to stay anon.,
But did she do it? Look!
Oh—Mrs.—Shepherd,
OH! MRS. SHEPHERD!
I'll hunt you hither, I'll hunt you yon.
Did you really hope to remain anon.?
Didn't you know the chance you took
Making a pass at a poet's cook?

Oh, Mrs. S. of the Nutmeg State
No human shame she knew,
Her carnal appetites to sate,
Our home she walked into.
Oh—Mrs.—Shepherd!
OH! Mrs. SHEPHERD!
By hook and by crook and by telephone
You attempted to rape us of our own.
You ruptured the laws of God and man
And made a pass at Matilda Ann.

Then here's a health to Matilda Ann,
Whose soups are soundly peppered,
Whose commonest meats are godlike feats,
Who resisted Mrs. Shepherd.
But—Oh—Mrs.—Shepherd!
OH! Mrs. SHEPHERD!
You ruptured the laws of man and God
When in our kitchen you softly trod.
You tiptoed hither, you tiptoed yon,
You fondly hoped to remain anon.,
But householders all, the nation over,
Shall hear the name of the lawless rover
Who by telephone and by hook and crook
Attempted to alienate our cook.
Go back to your home in Danbury, Conn.,
And carry this curse to ponder on:
I hope that your soup is washy-wishy,
Your salad sandy, your butter fishy,
Your sirloins fried and your whitebait boiled,
Your omelettes burned and your sherbets oiled,
Till all your neighbors in Danbury, Conn.,
As they watch the Shepherds grow feeble and wan,
Say "She should have thought of the chance she took,
Making a pass at a poet's cook."

Ogden Nash

Design for October

Then I heard a voice saying:
Summer is gone!
Summer is ended.
It is done. It is gone.
No more at morning
Will you stir the fawn
Or see the blackbirds
Black on the lawn
Or hear the crying
Geese of the dawn.
Then in my window
Grave was I.
Gravely I watched
The summer die,
And the last of the crying
Geese go by.

Jake Falstaff

The Angel of Last Judgment

[NEW FOSDICK CHURCH]

Lonely he stands against a lonely sky
And lifts a stone horn to his lips of stone—
Angel of judgment. Were there music blown
From that mute mouth, the ageless earth and sea
Would split asunder, and eternity
Strike down through time like sudden lightning sown
From dark wind plumed with cloud; old graves would groan
And dust resume its ancient effigy.

Deaf to his trumpet, through their little day
Swarming securely, mortal midgets run
Along the crowded street toward beds of clay,
Safe in their smallness, while their special sun,
Blazing and brief, mortality's reproof,
Sends his gaunt shadow plunging down the roof!

Jean Batchelor

Art Shoppe

Art is a clothespin butterfly;
Art is a silk square, streaked with dye;
Art is a worsted-woven mouse;
Art is shellacked gourds for the house;
Art is a bird's egg, painted, blown;
Art is a doll to hide the phone;
Art is a scooped-out armadillo,
A rosebud, waxed, and a paper pillow.

Jean McLean

The Question Mark

Behold the wicked little barb
    Which catches fish in human garb
And yanks them back when they feel gay
    With "Will it last?" or "Does it pay?"
It fastens neatly in the gills
    Of those who have uncertain wills,
But even wily eels are caught
    Upon this bent pin of a thought.

Persis Greely Anderson

251

Commuter

Commuter—one who spends his life
In riding to and from his wife;
A man who shaves and takes a train
And then rides back to shave again.

E. B. White

New Inventions

An Englishman who lives in Harrow
Has built, I hear, a wheelless barrow.
And two devout and earnest Germans
Have made a book of pop-up sermons.

Clarence Day

XI. NOVEMBER: *Spinster of the year*

November

Away with vanity of Man!
  Now comes to visit here
The Maiden Aunt, the Puritan,
  The Spinster of the year.

She likes a world that's furnished plain,
  A sky that's clean and bare,
And garments eminently sane
  For her consistent wear.

Let others deck them as they please
  In frill and furbelow.
She scorns alike the fripperies
  Of flowers and of snow.

Her very speech is shrewd and slight,
  With innuendoes done;
And all of her is hard, thin light
  Or shadow sharp as sun.

Indifferent to the drifting leaf,
  And innocent of guile,
She scarcely knows there dwells a brief
  Enchantment in her smile.

So love her with a sparing love.
  That is her private fashion,
Who fears the August ardor of
  A demonstrated passion.

Yet love her somewhat. It is meet,
  And for our own defence,
After October to find sweet
  Her chilly common sense.

Phyllis McGinley

The Temptation of S. Simeon Stylites

Poor S. Simeon on his pillar
Felt the cold come chill and chiller.

In the heat of summer, he
Kept complete his chastity.

Hot and fierce up in the sky
Burned the day-star's furious eye.

Strong and sure the message fell.
Simeon swooned and thought of Hell.

Poor S. Simeon on his pillar
Felt the cold come chill and chiller,

Felt the ice on winter's breath—
Cold as virtue; cold as death.

Tempting thoughts in Simeon's head:
Woman's warming flesh in bed;

Sin that makes the blood run hot;
Jungle nights of warmth and rot;

Wine: its warm taste and its smell;
Then: the grateful heat of Hell!

In the heat of summer, he
Kept complete his chastity:

Simeon, when winter fell,
Thought a kindly thought of Hell.

Jake Falstaff

Autres Bêtes, Autres Mœurs

I

The fish, when he's exposed to air,
Can show no trace of savoir-faire,
But in the sea regains his balance
And exploits all his many talents.
The chastest of the vertebrates,
He never even sees his mates,
But when they've finished, he appears
And O.K.'s all their bright ideas.

II

The turtle lives twixt plated decks
Which practically conceal its sex.
I think it clever of the turtle
In such a fix to be so fertile.

Ogden Nash

Complex, with Victim Victorious

M M

I have no homeland;
  I have no Saviour;
I live among people
  Of different behaviour;
I have no army,
  I have no navy
To rattle their victories,
  Stand by, and save me.

When I make blunders
  Of act or omission,
I have no aegis
  Of custom, tradition—

Chiefs or apostles
    To ward off the dangers:
When I am strange,
    I am strange among strangers.

Oh, to be different
    Breeds heartache and trouble!
But he who is strange
    Among strangers pays double.
I have no banner
    To fly from my passion,
No gentry to set
    My caprices in fashion.

For a half-note of music
    I stole from the spheres,
I must weep double
    The alien's tears;
I must be two times
    The stranger, it seems—
Once for my people,
    And once for my dreams.

For a petal of beauty
    I shook from the tree
Whose leaves are the moonlight,
    Whose roots are the sea,
I stand in the thunder-still
    Darkness and strip
For death without burial
    And love with a whip.

The lover who follows
    The feet of the spheres,
Shall wrestle with shadows
    And die on their spears;

But woe to him doubly,
    And double his loss,
If he have nor an army,
    A navy, a Cross!

An army and navy
    To fight for the Lord,
And acres and customs
    Enriched by the sword—
His music will dwindle,
    His petal will die,
And he may not take it
    As lightly as I.

                    Samuel Hoffenstein

Without All Due Respect

Mr. Arthur Brisbane
Considers his country's bane his bane,
He vigorously combats disloyalty,
And deprecates royalty,
And though his speech is somewhat informal,
He is a staunch advocate of the normal.
He can pen an editorial
As noble and succinct as the Lincoln Memorial
And in his column, which is widely syndicated,
The man in the street is vindicated.
Because he thought of putting LITTLE words in BIG letters,
He is now one of our betters.
He can sit for hour after hour
In a tastily gotten-up flat in the Ritz Tower,
Of which he is owner and proprietor
Because he is such a good wrietor.
I wonder if you and I could assume similar attitudes
If we too knew how to pound the multitude with platitudes.

                    Ogden Nash

Apparitions

Like clouds that casually come,
the forms of those we love,
some bright, some shadowy, and some
the color of the dove.

Half-realized by us, they fare
and, never fully seen,
in changing currents of the air,
present a varied mien.

How different the look of one
at midnight from at noon,
illumined by the sane sun
or by the foolish moon.

Peggy Bacon

Sketch for a Portrait

How calm she is, with her well-furnished soul
Equipped with light to search reluctant faces!
From any part she will contrive the Whole.
She talks of peril from the yellow races
And sends a contribution to Shanghai
Establishing her credit with the fates.
She finds in poetry an alibi,
And loves the line that only stands and waits:
Or she will quote you Browning . . . the wise thrush!
Along her conversation Pippa passes.
Angles she deprecates, preferring plush:
And she will turn on heaven astonished glasses
Nights when the sprawling meteors let fly . . .
She does not like me and I wonder why?

Grace Hazard Conkling

It Rolls On

This is the time of wonder, it is written;
  Man has undone the ultimate mysteries.
  (We turn from the Chrysler Tower to watch a kitten,
  Turn to a dead fish from Isocrates;
Drinkers on five day boats are gladly smitten
  Unconscious on the subjugated seas;
  Einstein is even more dull than Bulwer-Lytton;
  You cannot smoke on the *Los Angeles*.)
Science no longer knows the verb-form "can't,"
  Fresh meat will soon be shipped by radio;
  Scholars are harnessing the urgent ant
And making monstrous bastard fruits to grow,
  Building machines for things I do not want,
  Discovering truths I do not care to know.

                       Morris Bishop

For Serena, Who Owns a Pair of Snowshoes

    Across my heart, in little strides,
      In little high-heeled slippers,
    You walk, in whom no need resides
      For overshoes or zippers.

    The paths across my heart, you know,
      Are warm as any garden,
    And footwear, since I love you so,
      Need never be a burden.

    And even should my heart grow cold,
      With drifts too deep for *low* shoes,
    I think I'd need you, as of old—
      And you could wear your snowshoes.

                       E. B. White

The Mesecks

RESPECTFULLY DEDICATED TO THE MESECK TOWING LINE

Swaggering up the harbor,
    With Quarantine left behind you,
Your liner stops and tootles for help,
    And who comes out to find you?
Who comes out to help you
    But Mesecks all in a flock—
A fleet of little Mesecks,
Of hovering, anxious Mesecks,
Of scurrying tugboat Mesecks,
    To waggle you into dock.

Walter Meseck, and Bessie Meseck, and Meseck, Carrie T.,
Margaret, Madeline, William Meseck, and Meseck, Mary E.

I've never come up the harbor
    At the end of a six days' journey
But the Meseck names have taken my gaze
    Like unknown knights at a tourney.
Mary and Bessie and Carrie,
    Madeline, Walter, and Bill—
What are they like, those Mesecks,
Those veiled, mysterious Mesecks,
Those secret, glamorous Mesecks
    Whose navies are never still?

Walter Meseck, and Bessie Meseck, and Meseck, Carrie T.,
Margaret, Madeline, William Meseck, and Meseck, Mary E.

I never have met the Mesecks
    —Though I pray that they're hale and hearty—
And I'm never a guest at a dinner
    Or a large, superior party

262

But I hope that my host or hostess
  Will hail me before I go
With "Haven't you met the Mesecks?
Come here and meet the Mesecks,
Come here and meet *all* the Mesecks,
  They're *such* nice people to know:

Walter Meseck, and Bessie Meseck, and Meseck, Carrie T.,
Margaret, Madeline, William Meseck, and Meseck, Mary E."

Kenneth Allan Robinson

On Learning That the Reservoir Is To Be Obliterated

[WITH APOLOGIES TO ELIA]

I knew a city, oh, I knew Manhattan,
In my days of childhood, in my joyful school-days—
All, all are gone, the old familiar landmarks.

I have been laughing, I have been coquetting,
Primping late, preening late, there in Peacock Alley—
All, all are gone, the old familiar landmarks.

I knew a square once, pleasantest of plazas:
Rapt is its golden girl, the Garden brick-dust;
All, all are gone, the old familiar landmarks.

I have a friend, a kinder friend has no one:
Like an ingrate, I left my friend abruptly;
Left him, to muse on the old familiar landmarks.

Ghost-like I paced round the haunts of my childhood,
Paused at the reservoir, soon to be earth-choked,
Soon to be lost with the old familiar landmarks.

Friend of my bosom, thou more than a brother,
Why wert not thou born in my own Manhattan?
So might we talk of the old familiar landmarks—

How some have changed, and some been disfigured,
And some erased forever; all are departed;
All, all are gone, the old familiar landmarks.

Babette Deutsch

Accident

A pool of bright blood, like the rain
That once on Pharaoh's Egypt fell,
Inexplicably scarlet lies
Upon the leaden city lane.
Huddled about it vulture-wise
Men stare as if a king again
Had from her height cast Jezebel.

Between gray walls and gutters gray
There flames this single gleam alone
Of color tragically shed
In splendor on the sordid stone.
Dull eyes from which desire has fled
Behold before them on the way
The sacramental wine and bread.

Amazed, men find before their feet
Beauty poured perilously near
Transforming the familiar street.
A pang of unaccustomed fear
Troubles their quiet, careless breath,
Nor do they know that life is here
Less lovely than the step of death.

Jean Batchelor

264

Late Autumn

Rafters of ice now wedge the brittle reeds.
The cold, banked air has let the dry leaves fall
And the black-browed bird has shaken
Without hope all the empty-podded weeds.
The quivering rabbit lies beneath the wall.
The frozen apple bends its bough untaken.

Winter will come, as this bright autumn came.
The cobweb silver twigs against the hill
Will catch the snow and spill it stem by stem
Upon heaped leaves that none would chide or blame
For having shrivelled, on the roots that still
Are maple roots though change drift over them.

Be brave. Change does not matter. None are wise,
But all are fortunate, and fortune falls
Least on the careful mind, most on the heart
Content with repetition, on the eyes
That dare look often at the same four walls,
The same four seasons ending where they start.

Raymond Holden

November

Say what you like and say what you will,
    This is an end of decent weather;
The green hide molts from the God-damned hill
    And summer and beauty stalk off together.

Dawn will come late and still too early,
    The imbecile wind will have shutters to pound,
And the best of me will go sullen and surly
    With the bear and the woodchuck into the ground.

Jake Falstaff

265

But Not Forgotten

I think, no matter where you stray,
That I shall go with you a way.
Though you may wander fairer lands,
You will not soon forget my hands,
Nor yet the way I held my head,
Nor all the tremulous things I said.
You still will see me, small and white
And smiling, in the secret night,
And feel my arms about you when
The dawn comes fluttering back again.
I think, no matter where you be,
You'll hold me in your memory
And keep my image, there without me,
By telling later loves about me.

Dorothy Parker

Incurable

And if my heart be scarred and burned,
The safer, I, for all I learned;
The calmer, I, to see it true
That ways of love are never new—
The love that sets you daft and dazed
Is every love that ever blazed;
The happier, I, to fathom this:
A kiss is every other kiss.
The reckless vow, the lovely name,
When Helen walked, were spoke the same;
The weighted breast, the grinding woe,
When Phaon fled, were ever so.
Oh, it is sure as it is sad

That any lad is every lad,
And what's a girl, to dare implore
Her dear be hers forevermore?
Though he be tried and he be bold,
And swearing death should he be cold,
He'll run the path the others went. . . .
But you, my sweet, are different.

Dorothy Parker

Melancholy Reflections After a Lost Argument

I always pay the verbal score
    With wit, concise, selective.
I have an apt and ample store
    Of ladylike invective.

My mots, retorts, and quips of speech,
    Hilarious or solemn,
Placed end to end, no doubt, would reach
    To any gossip column.

But what avails the epigram,
    The clever and the clear shot,
Invented chiefly when I am
    The only one in earshot?

And where's the good of repartee
    To quell a hostile laughter,
That tardily occurs to me
    A half an hour after?

God rest you merry, gentlemen,
    Who nastily have caught
The art of always striking when
    The irony is hot.

Phyllis McGinley

Song Out of a Rainy Night

What strange small moon hid
In the quick-darkened hollow
Of a hill's arm? Did
A wet wind harvest the stars, rain follow?

What was there in poplars bent to a whirl of wind,
In leaves slit
From the stem by the daggered rain,
To fill a man with tumult, to shake a stain
Of lost-moon-colored notes
Out of thin
Darkness, out of a man's hidden and hemlock-bitter throat?

Frances Frost

Three-Volume Novel

Talking of books and life, you said lightly—
In the way of talk, with the worn phrase, the fumbling
Makeshift word, and the dagger-dart of a sprightly
Insight, with words forever building and crumbling—

You said of a situation whose implications
Wandered as wide as cowpaths over a meadow
That a certain human life in its mixed relations
Loomed like a monolith, cast a gigantic shadow.

And I thought of lives I had known that adumbrated
More than will ever be known, till writing and printing
Seemed flimsy lath in the face of life created,
Or mere cold clay adorned with a little tinting.

Image-makers, dupes of the hieroglyphic,
Slaves of words perpetually wreathing

268

Quick, actual life—the one and only specific
For human despair, the thing that is living and breathing—

What pyramids of tomes we have raised to puzzle
Its meaning forth, and to voice our praise or censure,
When the warmth of a woman's breast, or a dog's muzzle,
Can swerve our histories into real adventure

Deep and wide and strange as all intuition,
With circumstance in infinite, intricate linking!
So we address us to ink, and the mild perdition
Of aping life with something we call our thinking.

William Rose Benét

Text for a Sampler

The lovely queen, Semiramis, when she made up her mind
She'd had enough of general, corporal, sentry, prince,
Enough of Hanging Gardens, and enough
Of pearls sewn thick as stars on silken stuff,
Enough of subtle poisoning of lovers overbold,
In brief, when Queen Semiramis was growing somewhat cold,
She took a walk one evening, and with not a look behind
She grimly kept on walking and she's not been heard from since.

They sought her in the palace, they searched the city o'er,
"Semiramis! Semiramis!" In market, street, and fair,
Babylon is calling "Semiramis, come back!"
Babylon is draping her balconies in black.
As fainter grew the calling, the legend grew apace,
About the lady's beauty of hair and eyes and face.
But—I think it takes a weary queen to slam a palace door,
And it takes a witty woman to give herself the air.

Ellen McLoughlin

269

City Songs

I

What if the ways be stone,
  What if the many pass?
We are to lie alone
  Behind a curtained glass.

What if the wheels be swift,
  What if the horns be loud?
Here is the corner; lift
  Your lashes out of the crowd.

Let them flutter and crawl
  To the nineteenth window up.
We are to light a small,
  Circular fire and sup.

Two yellow lamps, and a blue
  Circular flame to start.
After we can do
  With darkness, heart on heart.

II

Think no less of all his pain
  Because he told it in a room.
The song he sang and the refrain
  Are old as air, and dark as doom.

Such an old unhappiness
  Was not for half the sky to hear.
Walls remember our distress;
  Floors are pitiful of fear.

The winds receive our song and go.
His was kept, and is the same
As when you held your forehead low
To catch the syllables that came.

Think no less of any word
Because it filled a little room.
That night is gone, but we have heard
Eternal singing in a tomb.

Mark Van Doren

Fatigue

The man in the corner
all slumped over
looks forlorner
than a tired lover,

forehead dulled
with heavy working,
eyelids lulled
by the train's jerking;

head hangs noddy,
limbs go limply,
among a number
he dozes simply;

a dumb slumber,
a dead ending,
a spent body
homeward wending.

Peggy Bacon

Apprehensive Survey

OF THE POETRY SITUATION SINCE SUCH STALWARTS AS ENGLE
ET AL. HAVE PROVED THE GOSPEL OF AFFIRMATION
TO BE SO COMMERCIALLY SUCCESSFUL

With sound of fife and trumpet, with roll of pulsing drum,
From school and town and prairie, I hear the poets come—
The young, the clean-limbed poets, seers of the newer day,
In black italics singing the Everlasting Yea.

Glory, glory, honor and grace
To the latest thing in the market place!
Honey and milk and royalties give
To boys who hymn the Affirmative,
For the world is dark
  And the world is hard
And eager to hark
  To a bouncing bard
Who'll flaunt the laurel and not the rue.
But what are the rest of us going to do?

They flex their mighty muscles to greet the rosy morn.
They're ploughing up the Wasteland and planting it to corn.
And all their odes are hopeful ones and all their words corrective,
But what is to become of us who bartered in invective?

If poets must all turn loving and giving,
How in the world shall we make a living
Who went to a different, a ribald school,
Where looking askance was the permanent rule,
Who nodded a head
  Or raised an eyebrow
And earned our bread
  In the sweat of our high brow?
Oh, how can we learn in a single night
To sound as merry as Harold Bell Wright?

Come, dance upon the mountains and leap upon the hills.
Now chant the current doctrine that cures our ancient ills.
For all the glad young gentlemen are going forth to preach,
And we who loved the lemon must learn to suck the peach.

Pessimist poets, cease your wails.
Silence your mocking, drop your flails.
Set your feet on the good green sod.
Scatter sweetness and light abroad.
Labor, labor,
   With lusty song!
Love your neighbor
   And hate the wrong,
And strong and fierce as tiger whelps,
Plump for the Sunrise like Dr. Phelps.

Then, when you've finished the golden circuit,
Show the rest of us how to work it,
For the wind blows warm, the wind blows south,
It blows the bread right out of our mouth,
Who thought up a symbol to call a spade
And found frustration a likely trade.
A terrible word
   Is "Yes" to say
When you've long preferred
   A resonant "Nay,"
And your lips are stiff
   From their strict endeavor
To shape an "If"
   Or define a "Never."
And being expected to lift things up
Is bitter brew for us all to sup
When everyone knows, who has sought renown,
That it's much more amusing to knock things down.

Phyllis McGinley

Mary at the Fair
Or, Advice from a Gypsy

The ring's no more than parcel-gilt;
Folly to pretend it!
The cup is cracked, the milk is spilt;
Crying will not mend it:
Here's a pill you cannot sweeten;
Here's a frosted cake you've eaten;
A penny, and you've spent it.

Though they tie you to a cart
And whip you through the city,
He who never gave his heart
Will never give his pity;
Dry your tears; admit your error;
Kiss your mouth within the mirror;
Thank your stars you're pretty.

Mary, you have made your bed
Out of briars and withies;
No one lies where you are laid
For a score of prithees;
Pillow stuffed with stinging nettles
Harsh as adamantine metals
From the devil's smithies!

Mary, wait another year;
Turn your mattress over;
You shall see it change, my dear,
To a field of clover:
When the first hour of April opens—
Look, my lass, I'll lay you tuppence—
You shall find a lover.

Elinor Wylie

Hughie at the Inn
Or, Advice from a Tapster

Is it not fine to fling against loaded dice
Yet to win once or twice?
To bear a rusty sword without an edge
Yet wound the thief in the hedge?
To be unhorsed, and drown in horrid muck,
And in at the death, by luck?
To meet a masked assassin in a cape,
And kill him, and escape?
To have the usurers all your fortune take,
And a bare living make
By industry, and your brow's personal sweat?
To be caught in the bird-net
Of a bad marriage; then to be trepanned
And stranded on foreign land?
To be cast into prison damp and vile,
And break bars with a blunt file?
To be cut down from gallows while you breathe
And live, by the skin of your teeth?
To defy the tyrant world, and at a pinch
To wrest from it an inch?
To engage the stars in combat, and therefrom
Pluck a hair's breadth of room?
Is it not fine, worthy of Titans or gods,
To challenge such heavy odds?
But no, but no, my lad;
'Tis cruel chance gone mad;
A stab in the back; a serpent in the breast;
And worst that murders best.
Such broad and open affronts to fear and pain
Breed maggots in the brain;
They are not valor, but the merest rash
Rubbish and balderdash.
Fortune's a drab, and vice her native soil,

And the button's off her foil.
Season your ale, now these long nights draw in,
With thought to save your skin:
Be provident, and pray for cowardice
And the loaded pair of dice.

Elinor Wylie

Man Alone

It is yourself you seek,
In a long rage
Scanning through light and darkness
Mirrors, the page,

Where should reflected be
Those eyes and that thick hair,
That passionate look, that laughter.
You should appear

Within the book, or doubled,
Freed, in the silvered glass.
Into all other bodies
Yourself should pass.

The glass does not dissolve;
Like walls the mirrors stand.
The printed page gives back
Words by another hand;

And your infatuate eye
Meets not itself below:
Strangers lie in your arms,
As I lie now.

Louise Bogan

Will and Testament

I leave a little silver smile
　To shine for all the world to see;
Who deemed my friendship worth his while
　May have it as a legacy.
I give my hand to anyone
　If such with frankness he can take;
I will my eyes to look upon
　All Beauty for the Spirit's sake:
I wish my speech distributed
　To whosoever craves a word,
My song to be inherited
　By any pulse it may have stirred.
My Self is all I have to give,
　And I bequeath it while I live!

Persis Greely Anderson

Harvest of Half-Truths

Half the world revolves in sun,
　Half the world careens in shadow;
Whether light or dark is one
　With the bonedust and the mildew.

Summer wasps were nibs of life
　Till the hard frost stung the wing;
Half the flies are dead and safe,
　Half are cold as anything.

In the wry November light
　Much of goodly spring remains;
Dry the pond, and the frog's plight
　Stirs the reminiscent rains.

Turn us evenly in sun
  As the hausfrau browns the toast;
Half of us are underdone,
  Most of us are haply lost.

Half of us are devotees
  Of the nearest god that wakens,
Half of us are shooting peas
  At the stomachs of our ikons.

Half the populace are idle,
  Half are busy in a room;
All are gravebound from the cradle,
  All are hotfoot for their doom.

See the wise go wink-and-wink,
  Trading bits of heterodoxy,
While the simple sit and think
  In the amber nave of Roxy!

Half the world revolves in sun,
  With the other part in shadow;
Half a truth is worse than none,
  None is half of every credo.

Half the day destroys the tissue
  Half the night has built in sleep;
How can Man (half monkey) issue
  From the half-depths to the deep?
                              E. B. White

Solitary Observation Brought Back from A Short Sojourn in Hell

At midnight tears
Run into your ears.
              Louise Bogan

xii. DECEMBER: *We shall have snow*

I Want New York

I think those people are utterly unreliable
Who say they'd be happy on a desert island with a copy of the
Biable
And "Hamlet" (by Shakespeare) and "Don Quixote" (by
Cervantes)
And poems by Homer and Virgil and perhaps a thing or two
of Dante's.
And furthermore, I have a feeling that if they were marooned
till the millennium's dawn,
Very few of us would notice that they were gone.
Perhaps they don't like my opinions any better than I like theirs,
But who cares?
If I were going to be marooned and could take only one thing
along,
I'd be perfectly happy if I could take the thing which is the
subject of this song.
I don't mean anything that was brought either by the postman
or the stork.
I mean the City of New York.
For New York is a wonder city, a veritable fairyland
With many sights not to be seen in Massachusetts or Maryland.
It is situated on the island of Manhattan,
Which I prefer to such islands as Welfare or Staten.
And it is far superior
To the cities of the interior.
What if it has a heterogeneous populace?
That is one of the privileges of being a metropulace,
And heterogeneous people don't go round bothering each other,
And you can be reasonably sure that everything you do won't get
right back to your dear old mother.
In New York beautiful girls can become more beautiful by going
to Elizabeth Arden

And getting stuff put on their faces and waiting for it to harden,
And poor girls with nothing to their names but a letter or two
　　can get rich and joyous
From a brief trip to their lawyers.
And anybody with a relative of whose will he is the beneficiary
Can do pretty well in the judiciary.
So I can say with impunity
That New York is a city of opportunity.
It also has many fine theatres and hotels,
And a lot of taxis, buses, subways, and "L"s;
And anybody can find somewhere in it his favorite diversion,
Whether he be Argentine, Scandinavian, or Persian.
Best of all, if you don't show up at the office or at a tea nobody
　　will bother their head.
They will just think you are dead.
That's why I really think New York is exquisite.
It isn't all right just for a visit,
But by God's grace
I'd live in it and like it even better if they gave me the place.

Ogden Nash

Bulletin on the Simians

"What are they doing now?" I heard
One bird ask another bird.
"Talking away," the other said,
"Of what they hope and what they dread,
And how to manage their gold and drink,
And what a thinking man should think.
Some of them kneel in a church and pray,
Some of them sit at their books and dream,
Or button their clothes, or learn to play.
And none of them knows how odd they seem."

Clarence Day

Dog Around the Block

Dog around the block, sniff,
Hydrant sniffing, corner, grating,
Sniffing, always, starting forward,
Backward, dragging, sniffing backward,
Leash at taut, leash at dangle,
Leash in people's feet entangle—
Sniffing dog, apprised of smellings,
Love of life, and fronts of dwellings,
Meeting enemies,
Loving old acquaintance, sniff,
Sniffing hydrant for reminders,
Leg against the wall, raise,
Leaving grating, corner greeting,
Chance for meeting, sniff, meeting,
Meeting, telling, news of smelling,
Nose to tail, tail to nose,
Rigid, careful, pose,
Liking, partly liking, hating,
Then another hydrant, grating,
Leash at taut, leash at dangle,
Tangle, sniff, untangle,
Dog around the block, sniff.

E. B. White

Crossing the Color Line

Harlem
has a black belt
where darkies dwell
in a heaven
where white men
seek a little hell.
Alfred Kreymborg

To a Young Man Selecting Six Orchids

Tell me, brave young man, I pray,
Is she worth the price you pay?

You may think her quite sublime,
But take care while there is time.
Orchids lead to other things—
Satin ribbons, wedding rings,
Leases and refrigerators,
Apron strings, perambulators,
Cereal and safety pins,
Rice, and sometimes, even twins.

Tell me, brave young man, I pray,
Is she worth the price you pay?

Margaret Fishback

To Sad Young Women Who Bewail
In Verse the Sameness of the Male

Ladies of the acrid pen,
Celebrants of bored intriguing,
Having found the race of men
Flat, identical, fatiguing—
We admit that you describe us
Neatly when you diatribe us.

Apt, yet wistful, you bemoan
Masculine similitudeness,
Panning the male monotone
Bluntly, or with expert shrewdness;
Yet with all your repertory
You've omitted half the story.

Men, by cavalier tradition,
Can't express tart, similar woes;
Still, we have a mild suspicion
Every rose is—every rose;
Or, as Pat once said to Mike:
"All canaries sound alike."

Let us not anatomize
How and where you gals resemble
One another: swimming eyes,
Cheeks a-pale, and lips a-tremble;
But you must have heard the crack:
In the dark all cats are black!

When you swing upon your gate
Seeking love's next interview,
Pick a guy your size and weight,
Dry your eyes and see it through,
Remembering—for all its staleness—
Love knows just one kind of maleness!
                              Henry Morton Robinson

Hotel Lobby

Here's tropic flora
That astounds
The simple traveller.
Here abounds

The Mazda blossom,
By whose glare
Exotic fauna
Takes the air.

Amazing palms
Rear stalk on stalk

Where parrot pages
Strut and squawk

Unmindful
Of the eyes that burn
Behind the undergrowth
Of fern.

Off in the brush
A saxophone
Reiterates
The tribal moan.

A tom-tom throbs
An urgent plea.
The natives move
Uneasily.

With sullen grace
A leopard slinks
After a dashing pelt
Of lynx.

The jungle's stirring!
We will wait
For bigger game
To congregate.

Sequestered
On the mezzanine
We can observe
And be unseen.

Oh, strange
And awe-inspiring sight—
A jungle water-hole
By night!

Mildred Weston

286

Nocturne

Over New England now, the snow
glitters on spruce and applewood;
the white owl hunts by dusk where late
the rabbits found the autumn good.

In Pennsylvania, the tall
farmer brings in his final hay,
the second growth; his oxen plod
under the last cold green of day.

In Delaware, the stacks of corn
march like brown tepees on the sky.
In Maryland, by Havre de Grace,
the fishers spread their nets to dry.

Deep in Virginia, the blue
piled mountains hide the westward path,
and rivers hunting for the sea
are red as the sundown's aftermath.

The silver onslaught of the tide
assails the Carolina coast,
where the full boughs of sounding oaks
defy the faint approach of frost.

In Georgia, darkness grows along
the wandering pine-straw roads; the sweet
fragrance of landward wind lies down
with the small bright blades of winter wheat.

In Florida, hibiscus clench
their scarlet blooms beneath the stars,
while the sun-warmed beaches and the sea
thunder their slow, eternal wars.

Frances Frost

The Swan of the Heart

In the field the harrow
Stands without hands or horses,
Biting the frozen furrow.
In the watercourses
The water is white and slowed.
It is cold but it has not snowed.
The day is not dead but is dark
Under the hanging winter.
The hearth is a wavering spark,
The eaves-water a splinter.
Come down the mountain, come
You frosty-feathered cloud,
To this small-timbered home
Blowing, like frozen wool,
The rabbits to their crannies, cowed
And quivering, the pool
To iron, the column of the flue
To thunder. This hour was made for you
And your attempt. But look!
The blood is not a brook
To close upon itself and rear
A tree of clear
Black ice into the body's season;
Nor is the reason,
For its disquiet, subject to your shock
Behind its bony lock.
What, then, will your master,
Time, with his schemed disaster,
Say to defeat like yours—
To the summer that endures
Under the rabbit's pelt,
To the woman who can melt
The frozen hand between her sunny thighs?
What to the light unfrosted in the eyes,

To the memory and hope that go unarmed,
To the arrow of cold turned back, the swan of
the heart not harmed?

Raymond Holden

Hurrah for the Fun

A dinner without apricot liqueur is no dinner
at all.—*Elizabeth Hawes.*
A dinner without cognac brandy is simply un-
thinkable.—*Ilka Chase.*—Adv.

Over the river and through the woods,
  The guests are flocking fast,
To Grandma's roof for the pudding's proof
  And the holiday repast.
Oh, the pies smell lovely, Grandma.
  You're proud and you have just cause,
But what of the shears that shape careers,
  What of Elizabeth Hawes?
What if she turned up, Grandma?
  I'm sure you'd want to be right.
Let Fleurs Alpines remain unseen
  And Cointreau out of sight.
A dinner's never a dinner,
  In fact it is simply *not,*
If it should end with other blend
  Than one of apricot.
And let me caution you, Grandma—
  I'm sure that you'd want to know—
That just in case it were Ilka Chase,
  She won't want Curaçao,
Or Crème Yvette, or Anisette,
  Or others you have handy,
For she came clean in a magazine
  And said she wanted brandy.

Henrietta Fort Holland

Of All Things Difficult to Bear

Of all things difficult to bear,
Hunger and envy, love and thirst,
Sultry remorse and cold despair,
I hold this thing to be the worst—

After long journeying to lie
Down on some starless brink of space,
And put a question to the sky;
To know there lingers not a trace

Of what we were, in what we are;
And, weary to the soul, uproot
Our dearest dream as too bizarre
Ever to blossom or bear fruit.

Helene Mullins

Pullman

From each compartment, with its neat white number,
Arise the small occasional sounds of slumber . . .

The drowsy stir, the little sighs up-wreathing
Of human animals relaxed, soft-breathing.

Here, without question, is a most demure
Provision by whose grace they rest secure,

In such proximity so chastely laid,
Sleeping (ingenuous custom) man and maid

Inviolate, protected by a certain
Conventionality of drawn green curtain.

Sara Henderson Hay

Angel Infancy

Within the close the lawn is green and trim,
The wall of brick bright red with vines in view,
The clouds are lamb's wool upon eggshell blue;
The Dean, black-gaitered, has a mouth that's prim,
While round the bald gray-tufted head of him
Pink cherubs on their harps twang hallyloo,
Floating plump-limbed on air as cherubs do,
Or did when ladies never wore a limb.

Discreet in billowing crinolines and lace
And Balmorals and little buttoned boots,
The ladies sip and simper. Overhead,
Framed in a window, with jam upon his face,
A pudgy boy ingeniously makes snoots
At all below, wishing the Dean was dead.

The lavender decorum of the sky,
Paling toward evening, tints the scones and tea,
And all is sweetness and sobriety,
Save where an inspiration from on high
Has now impaled a large bluebottle fly
And lowered it on bent pin carefully
To where the dozing Dean—for it is he!—
Lets tir'd eyelid droop o'er tir'd eye.

O wild hosanna from that outraged nose,
O crinoline-flurry like a flowerbed bowed
Beneath the rainy gust from riven cloud,
O face suffused, each feature in what throes,
Where the tea-table with silver clash careens,
O glorious gaitered leap that is the Dean's!

The moon, that white-faced coachman of the brougham
Of night, drives high in heaven the dappled cloud,
While sofa'd parlors settle deep in shroud
Of shadow. Under eaves, an urchin's room
Fills with wild puckish fancies that beplume
Young anguish and disperse a phantom crowd
Of Deans with leathern straps, though night is loud
Now with cathedral chimes that roam and boom.

Thus, Blinkered Era of lugubrious joys,
In rose-filled closes dozing life away
Or, stiff in broadcloth and in bombazine,
Marching to church the God of little boys,
Your gloom I rifle of one heartening ray
Lighting a day of Tommy's with the Dean.

William Rose Benét

Harper to Mifflin to Chance

Among the authors who have recently gone to other publishers are
H. G. Wells, who left Doubleday Doran for Macmillan; Charles Morgan,
author of "The Fountain," who went to Macmillan from Knopf; Harold
Bell Wright, who left Appleton's for Harper's; Aldous Huxley, who left
Doubleday Doran for Harper's; Louis Bromfield, who left Stokes for
Harper's; Tiffany Thayer, who left Claude Kendall for Liveright; and
J. P. McEvoy, who went from Simon & Schuster to Houghton Mifflin.
—*The Times*.

Come Harper, come Schuster, come Appleton all,
The winter is coming, and gone is the fall,
The authors are restless and pining to go,
And Santa is poorly and we shall have snow!
  Come *on*, Harper!

Come Huxley, come Morgan, come Harold Bell Wright,
The dew's on the turnip—the publisher's blight;

Come Bromfield and Thayer, come all God's chillun,
Goodbye to Knopf, sir, and ho for Macmillan!
  Come *on*, Macmillan.

Ho ho! for the writers who pass in the night,
Hey hey! for Al Huxley and Harold Bell Wright,
For the moon on the crest of the new fallen snow
And the luster of Doubleday all in a row.
  Come *on*, Doubleday!

Come author, come poet, come scriveners bold,
The royalty's gone and the days grow cold,
So put on the imprint of Simon & Schuster
And sell a lot more than you formerly uster!
  Come *on*, Simon!

Come Appleton, Harper, come Mifflin and all!
To the top of the list, to the top of the wall!
Your authors are dressed in their last year's loyalty,
They'll kiss you goodbye for the first pretty royalty.
  Come *on*, Pater.

E. B. White

Farewell, My Friends

Farewell, my friends—farewell and hail!
I'm off to seek the Holy Grail.
  I cannot tell you why.
Remember, please, when I am gone,
'Twas Aspiration led me on.
Tiddlely-widdlely tootle-oo,
All I want is to stay with you,
  But here I go. Goodbye.

Clarence Day

Ward McAllister

Sherry with the terrapin and claret with the roast;
When the ladies leave the table, oh, it's then we love 'em most;
Madeira for the gentlemen to sit and drink their fill,
And Mr. Ward McAllister to lead in the quadrille!

Brownstone into marble is the way a city grows;
Marble into chrome and steel, and after, no one knows;
But brownstone into marble, as a thoughtful man will note,
Strolling to the Union Club with a flower in his coat.

The cotillion sets are forming to the airs from "Pinafore,"
And five-and-twenty Patriarchs will do to guard a door,
Before the brownstone crumbles and before the cries begin:
"Oh, Mr. Ward McAllister, it's time to let us in."

"Oh, wait a little longer, we'll be finished in a trice;
The figure's very pleasant and the dancing's very nice.
There's just enough of favors for the dancers on the floor,"
Quoth Mr. Ward McAllister, "and more is always more."

And what would be the favors for a leader in the dance?
A coat that's cut in Savile Row, a beard that's cut in France,
A corner at Delmonico's with the cover freshly laid,
And the choicest seat beside the whip in the Coaching Club
    Parade.

A pretty taste in canvasbacks, a taking way with whist,
A proper word on New Year's Day for every hand that's kissed;
A house in Twenty-first Street for a gentleman's abode,
And bayberry and goldenrod to line a Newport road.

Oh, Newport is a summer town with garlands on her brow,
But who drives a basket phaëton at noon in Newport now?
In Narragansett Avenue, what lady stops to call:
"Oh, Mr. Ward McAllister, pray get us up a ball"?

And who in Twenty-first Street now comes rolling up to dine
With "Mr. Ward McAllister, pray let us taste your wine"?
Not even Mrs. Astor sends to set her royal task:
"Oh, Mr. Ward McAllister, please tell us whom to ask."

Brownstone into marble and cotillion into dust,
And dancer into less-than-dream and brightest blade to rust;
The doors are all unguarded; they are trampling on the stairs,
But Mr. Ward McAllister he neither heeds nor cares.

Sherry with the terrapin and claret with the roast;
When the ladies leave the table, oh, it's then we love 'em most;
Madeira for the gentlemen to sit and drink their fill,
And Mr. Ward McAllister to lead in the quadrille!

Kenneth Allan Robinson

Epigrams in a Cellar

1. CLOS VOUGEOT 1911

Clad in full velvet, enters Clos Vougeot,
   Of lineage that none but he forgets,
And with the grace that none but he can show
   Salutes you with a bunch of violets.

2. CHAMBERTIN 1911

Chambertin! Methinks, a whit superb—
   His bearing both inheritance and art:
Yet, argued with, remark the mien acerb—
   He hides a touch of satire in his heart.

3. CLOS VOUGEOT 1923

This Young Vougeot, as gay as Chaucer's Squire,
   Boyish in faults, for youth will always err;

But ah, what blend of tenderness and fire
  When this our Damoiseau becomes Seigneur.

4. CHABLIS MOUTONNE 1915

Lady, I think you are Chablis Moutonne,
  A miracle of ether and bouquet:
Such colour as men feast their eyes upon
  And then, too deeply troubled, look away.

5. CORTON 1915 (*With a dead spider, crystallized in white
limestone moistures, clinging to the bottle*)

And here lies Corton, which Arachne chose
  In the cold cellar, craving summer's heat,
And tried, and tried in vain, before she froze,
  To warm on you her chilly little feet.
So to your spark of sunshine she expressed
  More tribute than a hundred poets give:
On your dark shoulder let none break her rest,
  A perfect little ivory adjective.

6. POUILLY 1915

Pouilly, I vow, is Madame la Marquise,
  And when she enters let no wooer speak
But watch, with apprehension and unease
  That faint flush of dominion on her cheek.

7. TACHE ROMANEE 1915

Tâche Romanée, whose lure one may explain:
  Aristocrat in masquerade as wench—
See, underneath that purple gypsy stain
  The silken lip, so amorously French.

Oh, Nuits St. Georges! Saint George of ancient time,
  Saint George the strong embarrasser of dragons:
We also spear the reptile with a rhyme
  And celebrate his obsequy with flagons.

9. Musigny 1911

Musigny is the Muses' chosen bowl,
  Pure element of Plato in potation:
Sets body into dialogue with soul
  And rubricates their secret conversation.

Christopher Morley

Christmas Eve

At this moment in Mississippi
Red leaves linger, chrysanthemums smolder,
Late roses clamber pale but fragrant
Right across the porch's shoulder.
At this moment in Oklahoma
Mistletoe weighs down great branches,
Sumach glows a frosty crimson,
Bittersweet wreathes broken fences.
At this moment in the New York subway
Package-laden melancholy
Bears poinsettia, crumbling pine-sprays,
Everywhere the brand of holly.
At this moment in Puerto Rico
Great waves smashing, bright and riven,
Fling spray to shore in salty garlands
Spattering spider lily and tree of heaven.

Muna Lee

The Dark Christmas on Wildwood Road

'Twas Christmas Eve and bitter cold;
The west wind raked the frozen mold,
And flaws of snow, with scorpion whips,
Picked at myriad weatherstrips,
And scourged the lated reveller
In dream-enfolded Westchester.

In the little house on Wildwood Road
The unattended furnace glowed
And dimmed to ashen gray. Thereat
The punctual-fingered thermostat
Growled a command to draft and lever.
The furnace fire was out, however.

Out of the baleful midnight shine,
A little sour with early wine,
Mouthing the dregs of Christmas glee,
Came Mrs. D. and Mr. D.
"You'll have to fix the furnace, dear,"
Said she. He sought a wounding sneer,
And then disdained to answer thus
The obvious with the obvious.

He cleaned the ash pit with a frown,
With savage strokes he shook her down.
He found behind the fruit-room door
A box full of excelsior;
He found some scraps of barrel staving,
A broken chair his wife was saving.
He dribbled coal with skillful care;
Then, sleep-befuddled, climbed the stair.

And very early Christmas morn
Junior blew his Christmas horn,
And Mrs. D. said cheerily,

"A merry Christmas, Mr. D."
She dressed in rapid negligee
To fetch the joys of Christmas Day;
But soon returned, a dread surmise
Swimming in amazèd eyes.

"Oh, did you see, behind the door,
A box full of excelsior,
Containing, in its piny mass,
A goblet of Bohemian glass?
Oh, tell me that you did not throw—"
"Well, how the hell was I to know?"
"Oh, what a senseless thing to do!
The present I was giving you!
It was a strange and dusky red,
A masterpiece, the salesmen said.
You burned my present up!"
                              "Oh, come,
It seems to me a little dumb
To leave such things around where someone
Could burn them up!"
                              "So, I'm the dumb one!
Because I wanted to surprise you!
And *I'm* to blame! Oh, I despise you!
I sometimes wish I'd not been born!"
And Junior blew his Christmas horn.

The unrepentant furnace glowed
In the little house on Wildwood Road.
Thermostatically controlled,
The drafts checkmated heat and cold.
What thermostat can regulate
The heart in sorrow and in hate?

And all that red-eyed Christmas morn
Junior blew his clamorous horn.
                              Morris Bishop

299

The Three Little Christmas Carols

Once upon a time there was a nasty old man named Scrooge
whom nobody loved or wanted,

And it seems that he was haunted,

And brandy is the spirit of the grape and rye is the spirit of rye
and Scotch is the spirit of barley,

And the ghost that haunted Scrooge was the spirit of a man
named Marley,

And in the days before Marley was a ghost, he and Scrooge had
been partners and as thick as the former Crown Prince and
the former Kaiser,

Because each of them was a miser,

And they were unpopular with many

Because they skinned every flint and pinched every penny.

Now, at the time the story opens, Marley had been dead for
seven years,

But Scrooge, when he thought about him, didn't give way to
tears,

And he didn't have spots before the eyes or sinking spells or fits
of dizziness,

Because he was rather pleased than otherwise, because he had
inherited the business,

And the old firm was even better off than before Marley got his
come-uppance,

Because where Marley had pinched a penny, Scrooge pinched
tuppence.

So one Christmas Eve Scrooge was sitting in his office sourly
revelling in his miserly proclivities,

And he not only stayed there himself but made his clerk stay
there too, although everybody else in the city of London was
making ready for their Christmas festivities,

And when his nephew came to invite him to Christmas dinner
and wished him a Merry Christmas, he pretended not to hear it,

And then he said a lot of harsh things about Christmas in
general, and particularly about the Christmas spirit,

And when he finally gave the next day, which was Christmas,
off to his clerk, who was Bob Cratchit,
He did it with the graciousness of a man chopping one of his
own fingers off with a hatchet,
And eventually he growled his way home to his lair, which was
the top of a warehouse, where he lived all by himself,
And instead of thinking about Christmas, he thought about pelf,
And he sipped a little gruel,
And he economized on fuel.
My gracious, but wasn't he a grim, grisly, disagreeable old relic!
Even his best friends, of whom he had none, would hardly
presume to call him angelic.
Suddenly in walked the ghost of Jacob Marley,
And he didn't welcome it, but it said it wanted to have a parley.
But Scrooge was inhospitable to the wraith,
And said that it was just something he had eaten, no doubt, and
in it he had no faith,
But finally the ghost convinced him that it really was a ghost
with a wealth of gruesome detail and anecdote,
And then wasn't he a terror-stricken old Scrooge, though his icy
nature did not ordinarily on panic dote,
Because the ghost told him that since its death its life had been
abysmal,
And was constantly growing more and more dismal,
And Scrooge looked more and more horrible and cadaverous
As he heard about all the awful things that happen to the ghosts
of people whose lives were given up to avarice,
And indeed I think that even the Spartans at Thermopylae
Would have quailed to learn the ghastly fate of people who do
not celebrate Christmas properly,
So then the ghost told him that some very important spirits
indeed were coming to see him and they would come in three
installments, like a story being serialized,
And then the ghost floated out the window and dematerialized,
And it is a wonder that Scrooge got to bed without bursting a
blood vessel or straining a ligament,

Because he was in quite a predigament.

Well, his naturally frigid blood ran colder and colder,

And he kept wanting to do what is very difficult to do when you are lying in bed, and that is to look over your shoulder,

And he certainly was sorry that he had no mother to guide him,

And suddenly, there was the first important spirit standing beside him,

And that was the Spirit of Christmas Past, and it staged a spectacle as good as any ever produced by Cecil B. De Mille or Adolph Zukor,

Showing him the kind of Christmas he used to have before he became absorbed in lucre,

And next came the Spirit of Christmas Present,

And it staged another spectacle, which convinced him that everybody was having a very jolly Christmas without him and he was only cutting off his nose to spite his face by acting unpleasant,

And then came the last spirit, and it said he had to guess whether it was the ghost of Hamlet's father or Banquo's ghost or the ghost of Julius Caesar,

But anyhow if he didn't do something about Christmas right away, he would come to a bad end as sure as his name was Ebenezer,

And then all the three spirits danced around the cauldron and chanted

Double, double toil and trouble; fire burn, and cauldron bubble,

And anybody here who doesn't hurry up and get some Christmas spirit is going to get into trouble,

So Scrooge said he certainly would, but he would like to get some sleep now, and he thanked them for their warning,

And he was a different man when he woke up on Christmas morning,

And he sent Tiny Tim a turkey and subscribed to charities and raised Bob Cratchit's salary from fifteen shillings a week to sixteen and went and had dinner with his nephew and generally behaved like a prince,

And he never pinched any more pennies or skinned any more
flints.
So remember, everybody, that you will be gladder but wiser
If you stop being a miser,
And I hope none of us here will have to be haunted by ghosts
to remind us that Christmas is a specially nice time to be alive,
And I wish you all a very merry one, and a very happy 1935.

Ogden Nash

New York—December, 1931

The child's cough scratches at my heart, my head
Buzzes with rumors of war, appalling news
From China, and queer stories of men bred
In ant-hills which will overthrow the world.
Machines can split the atom, if you choose,
And hens turn into cocks, I have heard said.
This does not unsteady my pulses.
Thoughts are hurled
East, west, and up and down the universe,
But none so dizzying as the sitting still,
In lamplight, among friends
(The cough's not worse?),
And watching eyes beam, lips move, fingers drill
Gently upon the table . . .
Oh, clever, oh, kind!
Here time undoes itself, here we rehearse
A drama not debated by the mind,
And see in fair beginnings fairer ends.
Say children cry, with reason, and men die,
Unreasonably, say our hearts are torn
And our brains puzzled—miracles persist!
Not the halved atom nor the changeling bird,
But this, the dazzling moment, close and human,
That for long pain makes brief complete amends.

Babette Deutsch

I'm Going to Start in Writing Letters:
A Sob Ballad

I

'Twas New Year's Eve. A party
  Was madly under way
In honor of some show girls.
  The hosts were clubmen gay.
There was rich food, wine and music.
  There was dancing, laughter, song.
But near midnight it grew quiet;
  Then an old boy asked, "What's wrong?
Are you sweeties making pledges
  For the New Year? That's no fun.
Cheer up! More wine! This party
  Has only just begun."
Here one girl dropped her wine glass,
  And when her chum did cry,
"For Heaven's sakes, what is it, Dot?"
  She bravely did reply:

REFRAIN

"I'm going to start in writing letters
  On New Year's to mother and dad.
This life, I won't let cause me to forget
  The best friends that I ever had.
A new leaf, I vow I'll turn over.
  May God keep it clean, the New Year,
As the letters I write, back home every night
  To my loved ones so precious and dear."

II

Now as she finished speaking
  The bells New Year proclaimed.

But there were no glad greetings.
  Her words, them all had shamed.
Just silence, which was broken
  By a youth who'd long admired
The girl. "Come, Dot, we're leaving;
  You're all keyed up and tired."
They left. Once in his auto,
  He said, "Let's quit this life.
A ranch out west I've purchased.
  Let's go there—man and wife."
When she whispered, "I am willing,"
  He answered, "I was right.
I knew you were pure gold, dear,
  When you did say tonight:

REFRAIN

'I'm going to start in writing letters
  On New Year's to mother and dad.
This life, I won't let cause me to forget
  The best friends that I ever had.
A new leaf, I vow I'll turn over.
  May God keep it clean, the New Year,
As the letters I write, back home every night
  To my loved ones so precious and dear.' "

Clarence Knapp

To a Modernistic Christmas Tree

From what astounding forest,
    From what enchanted wood
Were you brought here to startle
    This mortal brotherhood?

What storms do you remember?
    What white and magic rain?
What glittering elves that sought you
    On wings of cellophane?

Did lacquered birds confide you
    Their eggs of colored glass?
And came there once a maiden
    Across the tinsel grass,

A slim, enameled princess,
    Forced cruelly to toil,
So that she wept, beneath you,
    Bright tears of silver-foil?
                        Phyllis McGinley

Street Scene

Far from Assisi
Here he stands
Where down a well
Of windowed walls
Most blessedly
The sunlight falls
Golden below.
His outstretched hands
Ask alms of none
But scatter bread
For doves that whirl

306

The wing-tossed light
In irised eddies
And make bright
An aureole
About his head.
His days have followed
Poverty
But not that other
Rule austere
Of abstinence,
For lurching here
He reels in rings
Unsteadily,
A battered old St. Francis,
Till police
Arrest him
For disturbing public peace.

Jean Batchelor

December Evening

Up from the frozen street the music drifts:
The song of a sunny southern island lifts
From a barrel-organ in the bitter dark
To stony walls whose yellow windows mark
The evening fires by which we sit and listen,
Dreaming of tawny coasts and sapphire seas
And stars that fly like birds into the trees.

The organ-man moves on. The night is cold;
The air is sharp with frost, the windows glisten,
The wind is rising and the year is old.

Frances Frost

INDEX OF AUTHORS

309

[209